PUB WALKS IN & AROUND THE NEW FOREST

PETER CARNE

First published in 1993 by
Ensign Publications
a division of Hampshire Books Ltd.,
2 Redcar Street,
Southampton SO1 5LL.

a b c d

Designed and typeset by Precinct Press.
Cover design by The Design Laboratory.
Publisher David Graves.
Cover photo. by Terry Heathcote.
Text photos. by Peter Carne.
Maps by Jack Street.
Printed in England by Romsey Printing Co., Chandlers Ford.

ISBN 185455 088 8

Also available in this series:
Pub Walks around Andover
Pub Walks around Farnham
Pub Walks around Salisbury
Pub Walks in the New Forest
Pub Walks around Winchester
Pub Walks around Basingstoke
Pub Walks around Portsmouth
Pub Walks on the Isle of Wight
Pub Walks around Southampton
Pub Walks around Bournemouth & Poole

Walk • # CONTENTS • **Page**

• INTRODUCTION •

The New Forest is one of Britain's most popular walking areas. At all times of the year, and in virtually all weathers, you will meet enthusiastic ramblers stepping it out in the ancient woodlands, along the gravel tracks and green rides, through the fenced plantations and over the breezy open heathlands, no matter how remote from the highways and the busier haunts of man.

Unspoilt country, scenic variety and unrivalled rural peace are here to be had for the asking, not only deep within the Forest itself but around its fringes. Besides sampling some of the best of the New Forest proper, the 20 walks selected for this book explore its fascinating borderland. Field paths, coastal areas, village byways and placid chalk downland all contribute their own delights, and every walk gives opportunities to learn something about the history of the communities encountered and the countryside traversed, adding much to the interest of each outing.

To fill your cup of contentment, each route starts and ends at a pub where you can eat, drink and relax in preparation for your ramble or after the circular walk is over. On some walks you can also enjoy a pint and a pie, or something more substantial, along the way, and the various pubs, with the facilities they offer, are described. New Forest hostelries and others near by are noted for warm hospitality and for the quality of their catering — and are well used to catering for walkers.

Essential details also included are how to get to the starting points of the walks either by car or public transport, a map reference giving the precise location of each, the approximate length of each walk and the minimum time to allow for covering them. In some cases alternative longer and shorter routes are described. The specially drawn route map with each walk should suffice to amplify route directions in the text but appropriate Ordnance Survey Landranger and Pathfinder maps are listed for those who may need them.

Except where otherwise indicated, waterproof footwear is always advisable and a stick is recommended, not least to help negotiate the occasional sticky patches, especially following wet weather. Finally, remember always to observe the Countryside Code — leave no litter, shut all gates, avoid straying from footpaths or other rights of way, keep dogs under strict control and take particular care to avoid disturbing farm animals or wildlife. Always behave in such a manner that those who live and work in the countryside will have no cause not to welcome your presence.

PETER CARNE
March 1993

Quiet Countryside near Cadnam

WALK 1
Up to 3 hours
5 miles
Walk begins page 7

Background to the Walk

Cadnam, first recorded in 1272 as 'Cadenham' and apparently meaning 'homestead or enclosure of a man called Cada', has been slow to develop into a recognisable village despite its antiquity as a placename. It is not even a separate parish but, like Ower, Winsor, Newbridge and Bartley, lies within the parish of Copythorne, the name of which means 'cropped thorn' and is thought to relate to the ancient practice of pollarding, which involved trimming off side branches of certain trees as winter feed for forest deer.

Whereas Copythorne proper lies just outside the present New Forest, Cadnam is right on the edge of it, with extensive, scenic woodlands flanking the roads on its southern approaches. Such remnants of old time forest peace as may have lingered until recently have been swept into oblivion since the coming of the motorway, which looms high on an embankment directly behind the Sir John Barleycorn Inn to provide a striking confrontation between things ancient and modern.

In 1964 the Forest's boundary was extended to take in extensive commonlands between Cadnam and West Wellow along with the common rights still exercised by local owners of livestock. You skirt one of these, Cadnam Common, on the outward stage of this walk, which brings you to the edge of Bramshaw before swinging south to Brook. Bramshaw, recorded as Bramessage in William the Conqueror's Domesday survey, probably means 'wood or copse with brambles' and is a Forest border community where, at any time of the year and not just in the autumn pannage season, you are likely to meet free-ranging pigs as well

Maps
Landranger 1:50,000
Sheets 184, 195 and 196
Pathfinder 1:25,000
Sheet SU 21/31
or Outdoor Leisure Map
Map Reference of Start/Finish
SU293136

How to get there
Cadnam lies just off the western end of M27 at the confluence of A31 from Romsey, Ferndown and Wimborne, A336 from Totton, A337 from Lyndhurst, and B3079 from Landford (joined by B3078 from Fordingbridge, which is joined in turn by B3080 from Downton). From Southampton head west along A3024, M271 and M27 to Cadnam, where you turn off and take the first exit. From Bournemouth follow the town centre bypass (Wessex Way), A338 and then eastbound A31 to the beginning of M27 at Cadnam and there filter left to take the third exit. From the roundabout at the intersection of A336 and A337 head north for a few yards to The White Hart, which has car parks at front and rear (leave your car in the rear one), or turn left alongside it to follow Old Romsey Road to a car parking area approaching the Sir John Barleycorn Inn, the latter's own car park being strictly for

customers. Cadnam is served by Solent Blue Line/Wilts & Dorset buses on service X2 between Southampton, Ringwood, Bournemouth and Poole and services 31/31A between Southampton, Totton and Lyndhurst.

Pub facilities
White Hart, Cadnam
This hostelry traces its history back to AD1448. An earlier hostelry is supposed to have been a stopping-off place for Purkess (or Purkis), the charcoal-burner, when on his way to Winchester with the body of William Rufus. At a much later time it was a place of call for stagecoaches plying between London and Plymouth. It claims a ghost which makes its presence felt by the smell of heavily scented flowers in the oldest part of the building. Some original beams in the building's structure go with locally handmade Bartley bricks. Opening hours are 1030ish to around 1600 and from 1800-2300 on weekdays and at the usual times (1200-1500 and 1900-2230) on Sundays. Home made traditional pub fare ranging from stews and casseroles in winter to salads in summer may be ordered between 1200-1400 and from1800 (1900 on Sundays) to 2100. Brews include Boddington's, Flower's Original and Ringwood Best Bitter as well as Whitbread Best Bitter, Mild Ale, Murphy's Irish Stout, Guinness and draught cider. Barbecues and a skittle alley are other attractions. Children may use the large garden and may be admitted to the back room. Coach parties are catered for and well-behaved

The White Hart, Cadnam

as ponies, cattle, donkeys and even sheep — watch out for them at sharp bends if you motor this way.

Between Bramshaw and Brook you pass through part of the Warren Estate. Warren's House, close to your route, is the home of the Crosthwaite-Eyre family, one of whose members, the late Sir Oliver Crosthwaite-Eyre, was New Forest MP for many years. The family owns Bramshaw Golf Club and The Bell Inn at Brook, where Sir Oliver was a familiar figure in the bar when taking time off from Parliamentary and other duties.

Brook, with its two pubs, several thatched dwellings and situation near the source of the Cadnam River, whence its name, is a typically pleasant New Forest hamlet at the junction of two B roads and of a lane which winds south through woods to Rufus's Stone, where the Red King is said to have died. The story of how he went hunting one August day with some of his courtiers and became victim of an arrow possibly meant for a stag, or perhaps a boar, and loosed by one Sir Walter Tyrrell, is one of the best known in England's history, as is that of his subsequent journey to Winchester on the cart of a man named Purkess. Another theory has it, though, that he met his death near Beaulieu, so perhaps other oft-related details are the fruits of some embroidering of the facts of what actually happened 900 years ago.

You head back to Cadnam by way of Bignell Wood, an ancient tract of timber which shares its name with that of a house tucked away in the trees by the Cadnam River roughly halfway between Cadnam and Brook. Bignell Wood, the house, was a home of Sir Arthur Conan Doyle, creator of Sherlock Holmes and author of several historical novels much less read now than his tales about the celebrated detective.

Walk 1

Distance: ***Allow 3 hours for this five mile walk.***
Assuming a start at the Sir John Barleycorn Inn, follow Old Romsey Road east for a few yards and then turn left to bridge the tree-shaded, gravel-bottomed Cadnam River. One of the smallest waterways in Hampshire to rate as a river, this receives Forest streams with names like King's Garn Gutter and Coalmeer Gutter before meandering north-east around Copythorne to Paultons Park, where it feeds a lake. Near Ower it ends its brief existence by merging its modest substance with that of the River Blackwater, a tributary of the Test.

The lane you now follow passes under the M27 and crosses a cattlegrid flanked by a gate for walkers and riders. It then continues pleasantly as a tree-bordered, hedged byway alongside which ponies graze the verges as a reminder that you are still within the New Forest's official confines as decreed by an Act of Parliament passed in 1964. Disregard a lane that soon angles sharply right for Newbridge and carry on to Springer's Farm. This lies on your right, just short of a fork of lanes where you bear right, with the buildings of Manor Farm on your left. The lane you now follow curves left before being joined from the right by a road signposted as leading to Storm's Farm only. Ignore the latter and carry on a few yards farther to where a house confronts you just to the right of where the public road becomes a private driveway leading on into Warren's Estate.

Just short of the house and its flanking open gateway fork right from the metalled road to follow a grass-centred track which is also a public footpath. Oak and holly-shaded banks enclose the unmetalled hollow lane you now follow north, downhill to where what

dogs on leads are not unwelcome.

Sir John Barleycorn, Cadnam
Tracing its history as far back as the 12th century and even farther, this well known inn could well be the oldest pub in Hampshire and is certainly one of the most picturesque with its roof and doorway overhangs of thatch and its long, low, whitewashed frontage. Purkess the charcoal burner is claimed to have actually lived here (or perhaps in a previous inn on the same site?). Brews include Flower's Original and Strong's Country. Food ranges from steaks and crab and lobster to humble steak and kidney pie — always a favourite — and may be ordered between 1200-1430 and between 1830 (1900 Sundays) and 2230 (2200 Sundays), opening hours being 1100-1500 and 1800-2300 and as usual on Sundays.

Green Dragon Inn, Brook
This pub is where historian Dr Crawford from Southampton University once heard two local countrymen talking in a dialect not far removed from pure Saxon. Locals as well as visitors still congregate in the tile-floored New Forest Bar, the other bar, with its adjoining restaurant area, being carpeted. The 600-years-old thatched building has been a pub for about a century and opens from 1000-1430 and 1800-2300 on weekdays and from 1200-1430 and 1900-2230 on Sundays. Food, all home made, may be ordered between 1200-1400 and 1830-2115 and ranges

from ploughman's, rolls and jacket potatoes to mixed grills, chicken Kiev, fillet plaice and salmon shanties (salmon and broccoli in a creamy sauce).

The Bell Inn, Brook
A few yards farther along the road beyond The Green Dragon is this luxuriously appointed hostelry with a comfortable restaurant, a bar with an inglenook fireplace and beamed bedrooms in its oldest part. Opened in 1797 by ancestors of the present owners, who also own the adjacent Bramshaw Golf Club with its two 18-hole courses, it specialises in good food, fine wines, and home comforts for residents.

Leafy lane north of Cadnam

soon becomes an earth track bridges a stream. Beyond this the tree-fringe broadens into woodland, with oak, beech, holly and bracken spreading scenically to your right and mature oaks and hollies flanking tall larches to your left. Where Cadnam Common's open spaces come into view through the trees to your right the track forks, the main one continuing ahead. You follow a less well-defined grass track left-handed to a metal gate alongside a stile where there is a yellow waymarking arrow. Here my companion and I found a seat to enjoy a picnic lunch.

Cross the stile to follow a green lane bordered by bracken and scrub, soon passing through an open gateway to skirt left-handed of what we found as a rubbish tip, with woodland to the right. The grass track here angles left to a metal gate flanked by two stiles. Cross the right-hand stile, where a notice says 'please keep to the public footpath', to enter a meadow in which you head diagonally away from the right-hand fence towards a clearly visible white metal gate on the meadow's far side. Blenman's Farm overlooks you from your right as you approach the metal gate, alongside which a dilapidated stile precedes a hedged and fenced grass track. This joins the lane serving Blenman's Farm, which leads you ahead to a public road, grass-verged and tree-lined as you follow it left-handed. Grazing sheep and copper beeches in fresh leaf shared the road's green margin as we headed now south-west for half-a-mile to Bramshaw's outskirts.

Just short of Stock's Cross, where the road you now follow crosses the Brook-Landford road, turn left past Stock's Cross Lodge and through two gateless gateways to follow a metalled driveway which is also a public footpath. Rhodo-

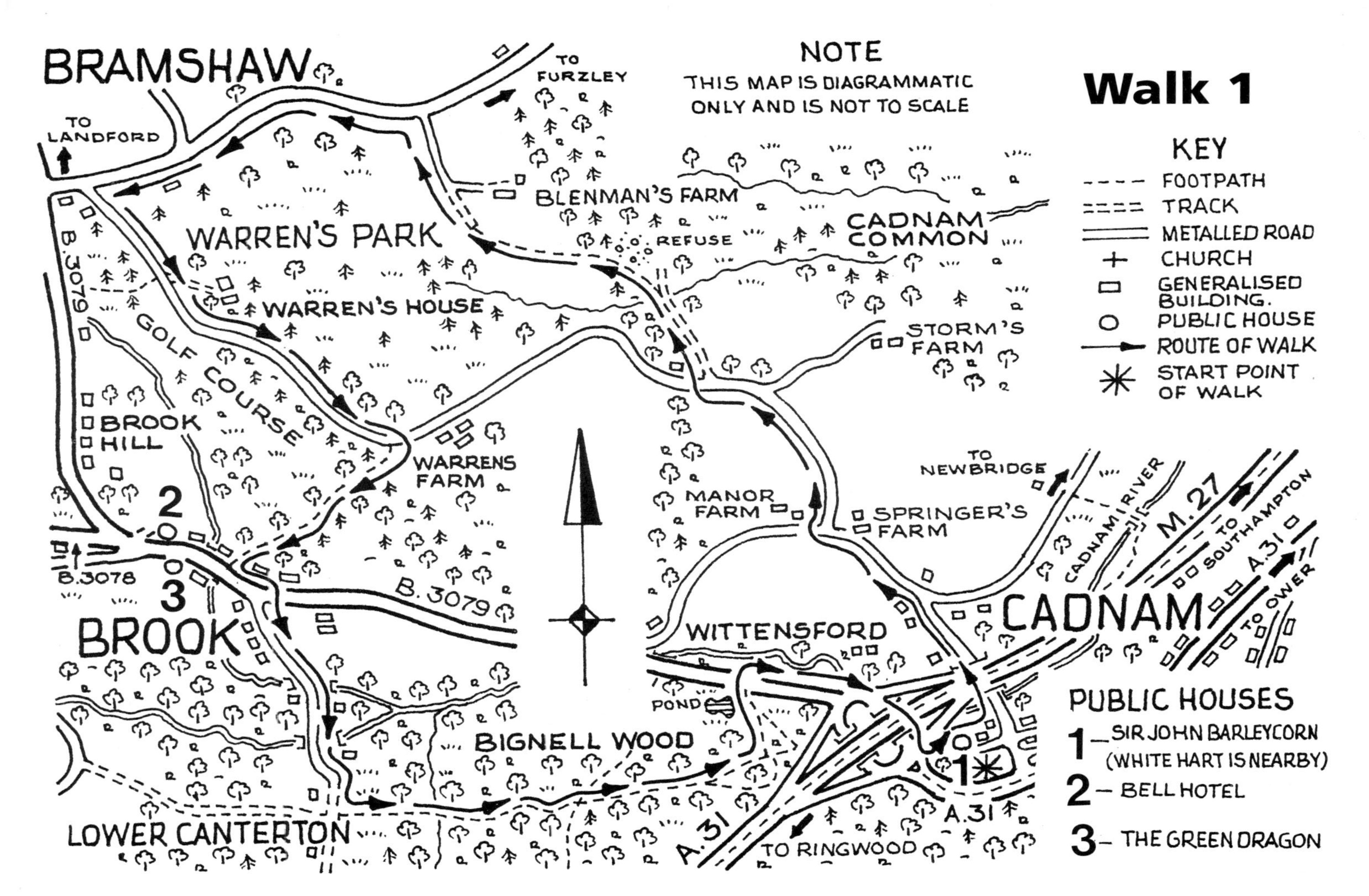

Walk 1
NOTE
THIS MAP IS DIAGRAMMATIC
ONLY AND IS NOT TO SCALE
KEY
FOOTPATH
TRACK
METALLED ROAD
CHURCH
GENERALISED BUILDING.
PUBLIC HOUSE
ROUTE OF WALK
START POINT OF WALK
BRAMSHAW
TO LANDFORD
TO FURZLEY
WARREN'S PARK
WARREN'S HOUSE
BLENMAN'S FARM
REFUSE
CADNAM COMMON
STORM'S FARM
B.3079
GOLF COURSE
BROOK HILL
WARRENS FARM
B.3078
B.3079
BROOK
MANOR FARM
SPRINGER'S FARM
TO NEWBRIDGE
CADNAM RIVER
M.27
TO SOUTHAMPTON
A.31
TO OWER
CADNAM
WITTENSFORD
POND
BIGNELL WOOD
LOWER CANTERTON
A.31
TO RINGWOOD
A.31
PUBLIC HOUSES
1 – SIR JOHN BARLEYCORN (WHITE HART IS NEARBY)
2 – BELL HOTEL
3 – THE GREEN DRAGON

The Sir John Barleycorn.

dendron-flanked parkland embellished with cedar now spreads beside you, with Warren's House in view through trees to your left as you head south-east past a right-hand golf course. A white metal gate flanked by a footpath sign on your right precedes a tree-lined earth and gravel track which leads you south-west, still alongside the golf course, to a wooden gate leading out on to B3079 at Brook. A few yards right-handed along this, beyond a stream and on your left, is The Green Dragon pub, while not much farther along, on your right, is the Bell Inn.

Returning from whichever of these is your choice for mid-walk refreshment, a few yards past where you joined B3079 fork right to follow an unfenced metalled lane. Houses alongside this precede bridges over two winding woodland brooks, beyond which you briefly ascend to open ground at Lower Canterton, a Forest hamlet well-hidden from the great wide world without. Opposite where a bridleway sign points right here you head left across a green to follow an easterly path through the old oaks, beeches and hollies of Bignell Wood, a beautiful tract of ancient timber where only the sound of A31 traffic through the trees not far to your right intrudes upon a pristine calm that can hardly have changed throughout the centuries. The fallow deer hoofprints that we saw here were of animals whose forebears have ranged these woods since Norman times.

Disregard crossing tracks as you head slightly north of east on a converging course with the ever busy A31. When you reach this turn left to make your way along a grass clearing, towards the end of which you skirt a small pond before emerging on to the unfenced B3079. Follow this road right-handed, under the end of the M3 motorway and so back to Cadnam and your car. The Sir John Barleycorn Inn lies to your left after you emerge from under the motorway and The White Hart is not far beyond.

Shady Ways around Woodlands, near Ashurst

WALK 2
Up to 3 hours
5½ miles
Walk begins page 13

Maps
Landranger 1:50,000
Sheet 196
Pathfinder 1:25,000
Sheet SU 21/31
or Outdoor Leisure Map
Map Reference of Start/Finish
SU324118

How to get there
Follow A3024, Totton's southern and western bypasses and A336 to Netley Marsh and there turn left if approaching from Southampton, or right if approaching from Bournemouth by way of Wessex Way, A338, A31 and Cadnam, to follow the Woodlands-signposted road. Within half a mile turn left from this and after a further very short distance you will reach The Gamekeeper pub on your left. Solent Blue Line/ Wilts & Dorset buses on service 31A between Southampton, Cadnam and Lyndhurst pass through Woodlands From Poole, Bournemouth and Ringwood take Solent Blue Line/Wilts & Dorset service X2 to Netley Marsh and either change to service 31A or walk for about a mile from there to Woodlands.

Background to the Walk

The Woodlands of today is not conspicuously wooded, being flanked on two sides by low-lying farmland sparsely interspersed with coppices of a size and number which might be expected in any agricultural area. Immediately to the south, though, spreads the New Forest, with woodland extending almost without a break to the outskirts of Lyndhurst and affording plenty of scope for leisurely exploration on foot.

Woodlands is not so much a village in its own right as a residential extension of Netley Marsh. Originally part of the once large parish of Eling, Netley Marsh, including Woodlands, became an independent parish in 1894, at a time when a good deal of building development was taking place in the area. A mere glance at Woodlands today reveals the 19th century origin of much of its housing, strung out as this is along both sides of the road from Netley Marsh and extending south-east along the New Forest's edge towards Ashurst. Apparently at one time there was plenty of thatch in the area, the reedbeds alongside the Test's lower reaches providing an abundant local supply of this material, but you will not see much thatch today. Redbridge, just over the Test where this joins salt water, derives from 'Reedbridge', experts tell us.

Many New Forest placenames are as picturesque as their origin is obscure. A good example is Busketts, the name of a tract of ancient woodland and of a forestry inclosure as well as part of the name of another plantation through which you pass in the course of this walk — Busketts Lawn Inclosure. Brockishill Inclosure, also on this route, is less mysterious, suggesting, as it does,

Pub facilities
Gamekeeper
Those who remember the Royal Oak pub at Woodlands of years gone by will find it now in a new guise as The Gamekeeper, a free house catering for both local and passing trade, and doing well. With its low, whitewashed front and hanging baskets of flowers in summer, the pub has a come-hither look about it from the moment you first catch sight of it. Real ales include Gale's HSB, Ringwood Forty-Niner, Ruddles County and Ruddles Best, and Gale's country wines are stocked. Two chefs are kept busy with the traditional home cooking which is one of the keys to the pub's popularity. Pies, pasties, grills, fish dishes and daily specials from the pantry menu are served in a separate dining area, while the bar menu offers basket meals and snacks. Sunday roasts are another attraction. Children may be brought into the dining area and the conservatory, and well-behaved dogs are tolerated. Summer barn dances are held in a marquee at the rear. There are no jukeboxes or pool table. Built in 1891 as a cottage, this has been a pub for a long time and an open, log-burning fire adds to winter comfort. New toilets have been added recently and the car park has been extended — ask first for permission to park here. Weekday opening times are 1100-1430 and 1800-2300, Sunday hours being 1200-1500 and 1900-2230 as usual. food may be ordered between 1200-1400 and between1830 (1900 on Sundays) and 2130.

an ancient haunt of Brock the badger, a well-established New Forest denizen. Brockishill precedes Furzy Lawn Inclosure, about whose meaning again there is no great mystery. Furze, or gorse, occurs abundantly on the more open parts of the Forest. In combination with the word 'lawn', which needs no erudite explanation, it hints at when the wood now so-called had yet to be established on what may well have been much more open ground.

Costicles Inclosure has a more intriguing name. Costicles Pond, next door, has been on the map for at least 200 years, during which time it has shrunk to a half-forgotten wooded swamp, though no doubt at one time it was important as a watering-place for cattle. Today the surrounding fenced woodland is supposed to exclude such animals. Anyway, the pond, with its name, pre-existed its namesake inclosure, which is nowadays just a hard-to-distinguish part of a block of plantations with no internal divisions to mark their once separate identities.

Accessible from three sides by busy roads, this tract of timber is a favourite haunt not just of ambitious walkers but of many who merely enjoy a gentle stroll not too far from their cars. Even so, there are quiet corners where you may still get a glimpse of deer. I have seen fallow deer and roe deer here and, once, the fresh tracks of a red deer, so you never know what you might meet around the next corner. I have also seen badgers, though not in the middle hours of the day when most people go walking. These are creatures of the night, which emerge at dusk when all is peaceful.

Winding through the heart of the woods is Bartley Water, a brown, mysterious brook which reaches the sea past Eling tide mill, a working museum open to visitors. At one time this miniature river served as a highway for the otter, a sleek, shy mammal which, alas, has all but gone from southern England. Today the odd heron, perhaps a grey wagtail or two and, in summer, gauzy-winged dragonflies are more likely to be seen if you diverge to follow the brook on its serpentine twistings among the trees.

The Gamekeeper

Walk 2

Distance: ***Allow 3 hours for a walk of five-and-a-half miles.***

Leaving the Gamekeeper pub at Woodlands behind you on your right, follow the cottage-flanked road for a very short distance to a brick-parapeted stream bridge flanked by a footpath sign. Turn left here to cross the first of five stiles with the tree-bordered brook alongside you at first. You follow the right-hand side of three successive small paddocks with intervening stiles to stile number four, beyond which a 3ft wide grass path leads you along a fenced corridor between fields. A plank footbridge and another footbridge with a handrail precede the fifth stile and your emergence on to a road where, looking back, you will see affixed to an oak tree a notice about the footpath you have just left. The notice requests that dogs be on a lead, and that footpath users should not loiter.

Follow the road left-handed for a few yards before passing through a metal gate on your left to follow a signposted bridleway: a grassy, tree-bordered track bordered in its turn by meadows bright with buttercups on the spring day when we walked here. A right-hand lily pond with an island was another eyecatching feature. Through a second gate you emerge on to Rossiters Lane, a track which you follow right-handed to emerge on to a metalled road.

Follow this cottage-bordered byway left-handed for a few hundred yards to a leftward bend by Goldenhayes, where you turn right-handed to follow a gravel track signposted as a bridleway. Carry on now to a double gate where a tributary track bends right. A left-hand pedestrian gate precedes a continuation of your own gravel track past a holiday caravan site. Gravel gives way to grass as you continue along a path with a strip of oak woodland on your right and hedged pastureland extending to the Forest edge on your left.

By a metal gate you enter what is officially the New Forest, with a scenic transformation at once immediate and spectacular. You now follow the right-hand edge of some picturesque ancient woodland, with cottages to your right. Beyond a vehicle barrier a gravel road leads on ahead, with fenced woodland to your left. A driveway between this wood and the Forest's edge precedes a road which you follow left-handed through open forest to a left-hand gate where you

Busketts Lawn Inclosure

enter Brockishill Inclosure. This fenced plantation was one of many created in the mid-19th century following the passing of an Act of Parliament designed to end the New Forest's days as a royal hunting ground. This measure, the Deer Removal Act of 1851, was only partially successful in achieving the aim embodied in its title, but very much more so in its allied purpose of enabling the Crown to fence off and plant up thousands of extra acres of once open Forest for growing timber. Brockishill Inclosure thus came into being in 1860.

Beech, oak, pine and other conifer species flank the gravel road you now follow south. Just over half-a-mile ahead, after bridging a stream, you enter Furzy Lawn Inclosure. At the next gravel track crossing you turn left to leave this inclosure by way of a double gate, the left-hand one of which is for pedestrians. You now follow a well-defined track through open forest. After crossing a stream culvert you keep right where a subsidiary track bears left and continue through old woodland of oak and beech to an open grassy area where tall pines are in view left-ahead.

Beyond an oak clump on your left follow an ill-defined wheel-marked track right-handed over open ground to join another wheel-marked track, which you follow left-handed through primeval-looking woodland. A reminder that you are not in fact very far from civilisation is a glimpse of a cricket ground just a few hundred yards to your left as you wind your way east to a double gate into Busketts Lawn Inclosure. Pass through the right-hand (pedestrian) gate to follow a rutted grass ride ahead. This brings you quickly to a track crossing from which a gravel road leads on ahead between tall pines and groves of oak, bending slightly

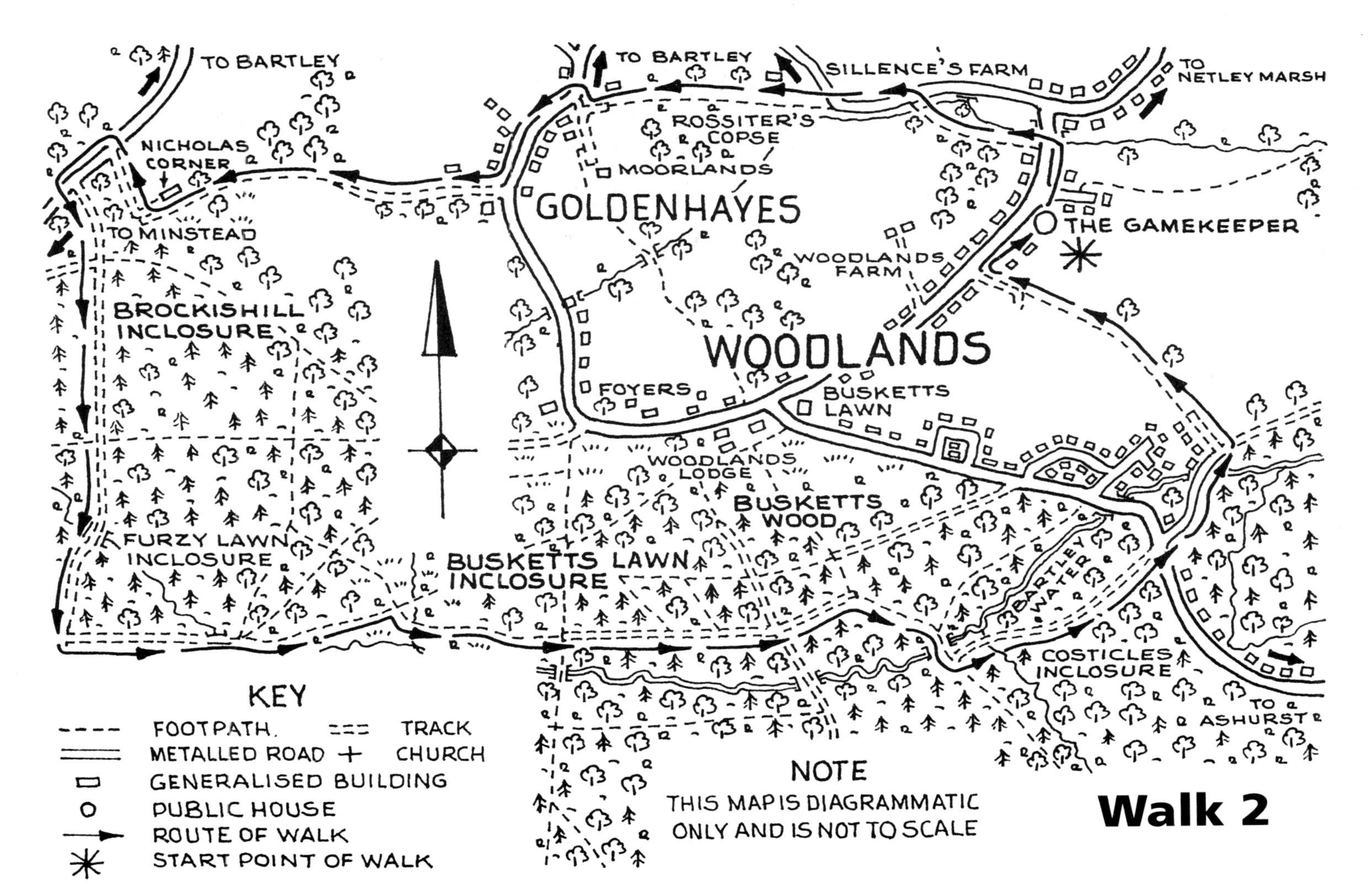

TO BARTLEY
NICHOLAS CORNER
TO MINSTEAD
BROCKISHILL INCLOSURE
FURZY LAWN INCLOSURE
TO BARTLEY
SILLENCE'S FARM
TO NETLEY MARSH
ROSSITER'S COPSE
MOORLANDS
GOLDENHAYES
THE GAMEKEEPER
WOODLANDS FARM
WOODLANDS
FOYERS
BUSKETTS LAWN
WOODLANDS LODGE
BUSKETTS WOOD
BUSKETTS LAWN INCLOSURE
BARTLEY WATER
COSTICLES INCLOSURE
TO ASHURST
KEY
FOOTPATH
TRACK
METALLED ROAD
CHURCH
GENERALISED BUILDING
PUBLIC HOUSE
ROUTE OF WALK
START POINT OF WALK
NOTE
THIS MAP IS DIAGRAMMATIC ONLY AND IS NOT TO SCALE
Walk 2

A forest walk near Bartley

left not far ahead where another gravel road turns right.

At the next gravel road junction turn right to cross a scenic stretch of the Bartley Water by a wooden footbridge alongside a ford. Trees here create a perpetual gloaming which enhances the rivulet's mystery as it twists and turns among them. Take the next left-turning gravel road through the mixed broadleafed trees and conifers of Costicles Inclosure.

Another double gate, the left-hand one being for pedestrian use, marks the point where you leave the New Forest. Cross a metalled road ahead, turning left and then right to follow Fletchwood Lane. This is macadamised as far as a bridge where you recross Bartley Water. A bridleway sign points ahead here. With privately-owned Fletchwood Copse to your right, follow a gravel road ahead to the far end of some bungalows, where a gravel drive leads you left-handed past more bungalows to a stile flanked by a footpath sign clustered with ivy when we passed it. Cross this to follow a hedged grass path between pastures towards Woodlands, directly ahead. Reaching the road here, follow it right-handed back to The Gamekeeper and your car.

Pinewoods and Heather near Hardley

WALK 3
Up to 3 hours
4 1/2 miles
Walk begins page 19

Background to the Walk

Perhaps surprisingly for so small a place in relation to the sizeable modern communities around it, Hardley has a history dating back to Norman times, when it rated a mention as 'Hardelie' in the Domesday survey. This derives from the Old English 'heard' and 'leah', meaning 'hard clearing' and therefore suggesting an island of human settlement amid surrounding wooded or waste land.

Hardley today is an industrial appendage of the lower Waterside area under the shadow of Fawley Refinery and is the first place you reach after skirting the New Forest by way of the busy A326. It links up in turn with Holbury, only a little way beyond which is populous Blackfield. Both of these last two places are modern developments largely created to accommodate those employed at the refinery and in the rash of satellite industries that have sprung up around the area, while Fawley itself retains at least something of the rural charm and atmosphere of times past.

The whole area was remote and inaccessible until the early years of the 20th century, when there was talk of constructing a railway — possibly to include access to the Isle of Wight by way of a tunnel under the Solent. There is a tradition that a causeway once existed between Lepe, on the Solent shore, and the Island opposite, this supposedly having been served by a Roman road from Eling — a road so named at Dibden Purlieu runs parallel with A326 and earthwork vestiges elsewhere correspond with the course of an ancient highway.

The railway idea was initially shelved in favour of a

Maps
Landranger 1:50,000
Sheet 196
Pathfinder 1:25,000
or Outdoor Leisure Map
Map Reference of Start/Finish
SU429049

How to get there
The Forest Home pub at Hardley lies on the left-hand side of A326, the Totton-Fawley road, a few yards in the Fawley direction as you approach from Hardley roundabout. To reach A326 from Southampton follow A3024 west out of the city and then A35 to the far end of Totton's southern bypass and there turn left. From the Bournemouth direction follow A35 and A337 via Christchurch to Lymington, and B3054 from there, bypassing Beaulieu village centre en route to Dibden Purlieu roundabout, where you join and follow right-handed A326 for nearly 2 miles. Take the second exit from the next roundabout, at Hardley, to reach The Forest Home on your left. Solent Blue Line buses on services 38 and X8 from Southampton, Totton and Hythe to Blackfield, Langley (and Lepe in summer) and services 39 and X9 from Southampton,

Totton and Hythe to Fawley/ Calshot pass The Forest Home. Bus access from Bournemouth is by Wilts & Dorset service 123 via Barton on Sea, New Milton and Milford-on-Sea to Lymington, connecting there with service 112 via Beaulieu to Hythe, where you change to one of the aforementioned buses from Southampton.

Pub facilities
The Forest Home
Open all day on weekdays from 1100-2300 and at the usual hours on Sundays, this Whitbread pub in Long Lane, Hardley, enjoys a busy lunchtime trade serving local industry and is a popular place of call at both lunchtimes and evenings for people from near and far. As well as the full range of Whitbread ales including bottled beers and lagers, a guest ale is always available, Gale's HSB having been choice of the month when I called, while a special offer was Poachers' Bitter at an astounding price. There is no formal food menu, dishes of the day being chalked up where all can see what is on offer. Hot pies, sausage dishes and a chef's special are always included, pub policy being to keep prices at around the £5 level or less. Traditional bar food listed when I called ranged from tasty rolls, chips, steak and kidney pie, fish and chips and scampi and chips to barbecue chicken, burgers, pasta, rump steak platter and traditional ploughman's, among much else. Food may be ordered between 1200-1430 on weekdays and Sundays and between 1900-2100 from

bus service, only to be revived in the 1920s when the oil industry and Fawley first came together. This happened when Anglo Gulf West Indies Petroleum Corporation (AGWI) built a refinery as a source of fuel oil for ships at a time when the big transatlantic liners and others were changing from coal to oil to heat their boilers. Bitumen for road improvements then commencing on an impressive scale was another AGWI product needing rail transport out of Fawley, and so, in the mid-Twenties, a line was at last constructed and opened — and not for refinery purposes only.

Five passenger trains each way on weekdays were soon whittled down to a skeleton service mainly for workmen. This lasted until the mid-Sixties, by which time Esso had taken over and hugely expanded Fawley Refinery. With its ancillary enterprises this now occupies most of what used to be Cadland Park, seat of the Drummond family from the 18th century onwards. Drummonds still own much land in the area, their home, the present Cadland House, being located close to the shore between Calshot and Lepe.

Apart from where it starts and finishes this is a Forest walk throughout, traversing formerly open heathland, part of which has been planted with trees. This came about following the New Forest Act of 1949, which made provision for the enclosure of additional acres of open land for timber production. These are known as Verderers' Inclosures from the fact that they could only be made with the approval of the New Forest Court of Verderers after careful consideration of proposals by the Forestry Commission in each individual case. Most of the eleven new plantations which resulted act as visual buffers between industry, busy roads and the like and the heartland of the Forest, as in the case of Fawley and Dibden Inclosures, traversed on this walk.

The open heath which remains, with its heather, gorse and scattered seedling pines, is a wilderness plateau grazed by ponies, affording habitat to the rare Dartford warbler and a few other birds, and inspiring widely differing reactions from different observers. In his *Rural Rides*, William Cobbett railed against its hostile, unproductive emptiness, which he likened to what

New Forest entry point from Hardley

Mondays to Saturdays, meals not being served on Sunday evenings. There is a garden with a play area for children, who are not allowed in the bars, nor are dogs. Walkers with muddy boots are welcome to use the public bar, and followers of this walk may leave their cars in the large pub car park. Pool, darts and electronic pub games are complemented by occasional live entertainment and there is a log fire in the winter.

he regarded as the ultimate in rural uselessness, Bagshot Heath in Surrey. In our overcrowded modern world one learns to appreciate such empty spaces as still remain for what they are, and Beaulieu Heath is one such space.

Walk 3

Distance: Allow up to 3 hours for this four-and-a-half mile walk.
From The Forest Home cross the road to follow a signposted bridleway which starts directly opposite. Fenced for its first few yards, this leads on along the right-hand edge of open ground with industrial premises to your right and brings you to another road, which you cross to follow another fenced section of the bridleway. Where you soon reach the end of the industrial complex the path bends at right-angles to the right, with industry still to your right. A landfill site lies to your left as you approach a tree-shaded wooden gate with pedestrian access alongside.

Here you enter the New Forest, passing straight from peripheral industry to a land of peace and ponies, not to mention other walkers, who make constant use of this area. Having stayed longer at the pub than we had initially intended, my companion and I used a Forest-edge bank as a seat for enjoying our picnic sandwiches. There is a proper seat not very many yards farther on.

This lies to the right of the well-defined grass footpath which bears half-left just beyond the gate towards the pines of Fawley Inclosure, which earlier formed a backdrop to the view across the landfill site. Long-needled Corsican pine and heather are the main features of this plantation, where the ground had to be ploughed to create a ridge-and-furrow base before trees could be successfully planted. You can still see where this was done as you proceed towards a point where the trees open out to present a view across a valley where a stream has broadened into a miniature lake.

On your way towards this you cross what the map shows as a linear earthwork running from north-west to south-east and pointing, in the latter direction, in a straight line towards Lepe. This is where the Roman road ended that was supposed to be linked with a ford making it possible to cross the Solent on foot when the tide was low, though it has to be said that there is not a shred of proof to back up this notion.

In the valley, below the miniature lake, which is really no more than a pool, you cross Dark Water stream by a wooden footbridge — Hardley Bridge. A few yards ahead, uphill, you reach the end of Fawley Inclosure and the beginning of Beaulieu Heath proper. Tracks divide here, with the right-hand one re-entering the wood. You keep left-ahead to pass through a former gateway and follow a track that gradually veers away from Fawley Inclosure, heading due west in an arrow-straight line across the heath.

Heather, gorse and the occasional stunted pine are virtually all that grow on this gravelly tableland. Apart from the odd, drab meadow pipit and a passing crow or two, bird-life is scarce in these surroundings, though the heath is home to at least one rarity. I remember being taken here with my wife many years ago to see my very first Dartford warbler. This long-tailed, little brown bird derives its popular name, 'fuzz-topper', from its habit of perching briefly atop a gorse bush before slipping away from view amid the prickles underneath in search of the spiders and other small prey upon which it subsists. Almost wiped out by severe winters in 1947 and 1963, this resident warbler has since recovered and re-established itself more securely on a handful of southern heathlands in the New Forest and elsewhere.

Ahead you will see traffic on the road between Hythe and Beaulieu as you strike west to follow the track across the heath. In case you should wonder why such a track exists, the reason becomes apparent once you cross the Beaulieu road, where a marker identifies the route followed by a gas pipeline from Fawley, buried underneath the gravel. Having crossed the road, carry on to a diagonal crossing of tracks about halfway between the road and the edge of woodland left-ahead. Bear right here and head north-west to the next track intersection. No fewer than six different tracks converge here. Take the fourth exit — in other words, the right-hand one of two tracks which both bear half-right — to skirt right-handed of a small birchwood and cross a dip to reach an open gateway at the southern end of Dibden Inclosure.

A twin to Fawley Inclosure in both origin and character, like the other it is no longer, strictly speaking, an inclosure. Trees having grown beyond the stage where browsing ponies can do much mischief, commoners' animals can now share this wood with the many local people and others who use it to walk their dogs, thanks to the facility of a car park.

Follow a gravel road ahead between pine plantations where both the Scots and the Corsican species may be found. Every so often grassy side paths penetrate the conifer gloom. For present purposes disregard them. At the first ride intersection

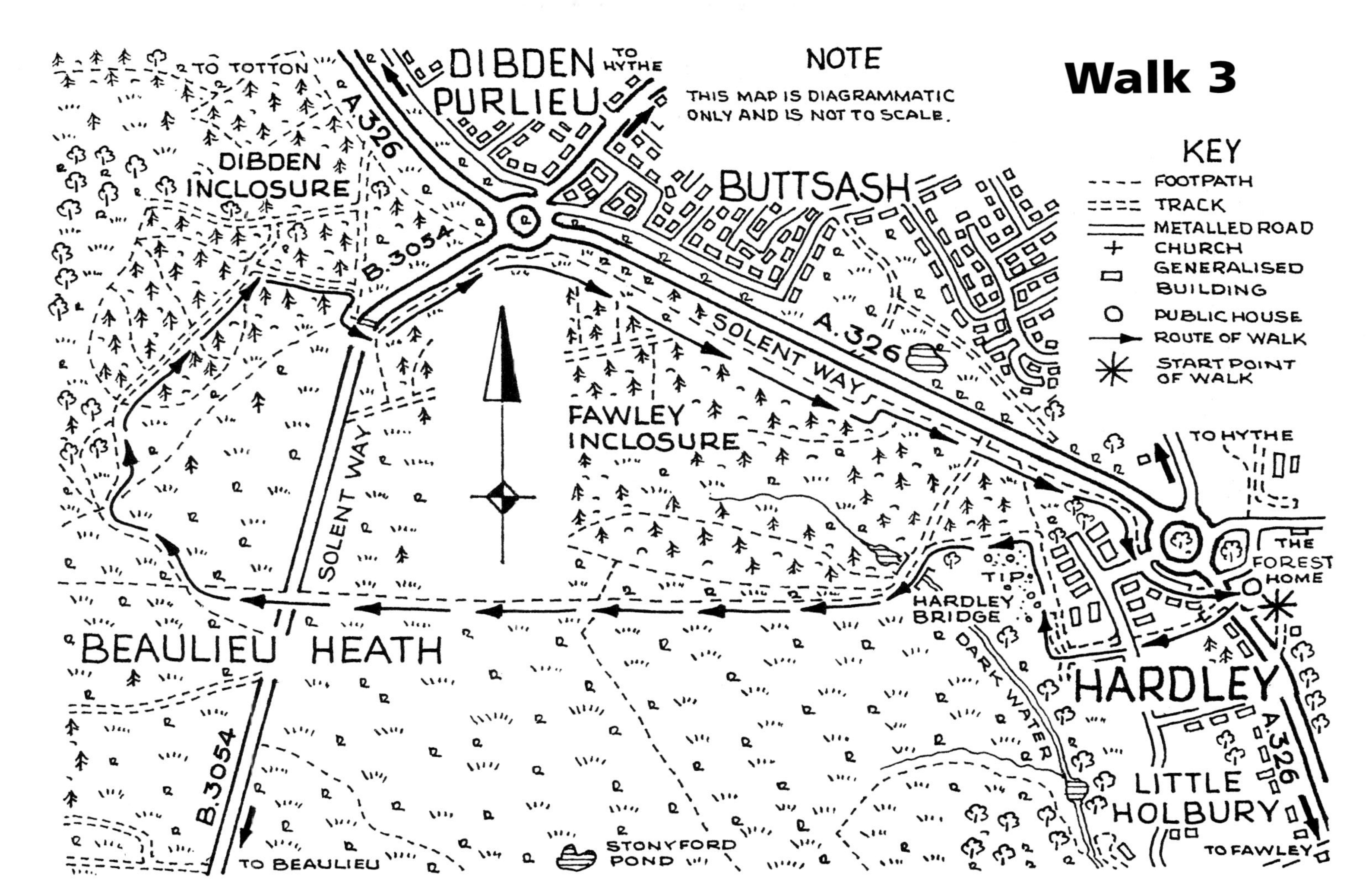

Walk 3
NOTE
THIS MAP IS DIAGRAMMATIC ONLY AND IS NOT TO SCALE.
KEY
FOOTPATH
TRACK
METALLED ROAD
CHURCH
GENERALISED BUILDING
PUBLIC HOUSE
ROUTE OF WALK
START POINT OF WALK
TO TOTTON
DIBDEN PURLIEU
TO HYTHE
A.326
DIBDEN INCLOSURE
B.3054
BUTTSASH
SOLENT WAY
A.326
FAWLEY INCLOSURE
SOLENT WAY
TO HYTHE
THE FOREST HOME
TIP
HARDLEY BRIDGE
DARK WATER
HARDLEY
A.326
LITTLE HOLBURY
TO FAWLEY
BEAULIEU HEATH
B.3054
TO BEAULIEU
STONYFORD POND

The Forest Home, Hardley

your gravelled way angles slightly right. Continue along it to a meeting point of five tracks in the woodland centre. Take the third exit to follow the main gravel road right-handed. A gate which is normally padlocked but with a pedestrian access adjoining precedes a car park and a second, open, gateway through which you emerge to reach the Hythe to Beaulieu road. Follow this right-handed through a gateway alongside a cattlegrid and then cross the road to join and follow left-handed what was a section of The Solent Way at the time when we tried this walk, and may still be.

This long distance walking route from Milford-on-Sea to Emsworth has been obliged by lack of footpaths to head inland and follow roads for much of the New Forest part of its course, as here just south of Dibden Purlieu. Its route, if it has not since been changed, runs parallel with the Beaulieu road, between the latter and Fawley Inclosure and with fences on both sides of it. At the time of writing it seems likely that means may be found of devising a route for The Solent Way through these parts which will follow fewer roads by steering a more southerly course. For present purposes follow the original Solent Way to within a very short distance of Dibden Purlieu roundabout. On the near side of a line of pylons and power lines turn right to follow a fairly wide clearing between the pines of Fawley Inclosure.

The obvious footpath following this clearing peters out where the latter angles slightly right. Turn left here to follow a gravelly path through the conifers for a few yards, emerging on to a parallel clearing which flanks the busy A326. Follow this right-handed to cross a footbridge and follow a track ahead, soon keeping left of a right-hand fence as you carry on to a New Forest boundary gate. Go through the adjoining pedestrian access to follow a continuation of the preceding track, the tree-bordered course of which leads to a metalled road. Cross this to carry on along Forest Lane to Hardley roundabout, directly beyond which you cross Long Lane to arrive back at The Forest Home.

Fields, Woods and Shore near Langley and Exbury

WALK 4
4 or 5 hours
6 ½ or 8 miles
Walk begins page 25

Background to the Walk

Between the New Forest and Southampton Water's western shoreline there was once a strip of quiet countryside largely forgotten by the outside world. Marchwood was unfeignedly rural, Hythe was an old world fishing village linked by ferry with Southampton but otherwise difficult of access, and Fawley was a byword for rustic remoteness and seclusion.

Then came a whole host of changes in the course of a few decades — aviation to Calshot, oil importation to Fawley, power boats to Hythe and much, much else that was destined to alter the face of the Waterside area virtually beyond recognition.

Yet this is not quite the whole story. On either side of Marchwood there are still green fields and leafy woods. Saltmarshes and remnants of inland verdure survive on the Fawley side of Hythe — and beyond now-populous Blackfield and neighbouring Langley you can still be right in the heart of the country as soon as you step off the metalled roads.

Langley's name echoes ancient rurality. Like that of its many namesakes in counties ranging from Wiltshire to Durham, it derives from Old English 'lang' and 'leah', meaning simply 'long wood or clearing'.

Earthwork traces of a road built by the Romans may still be seen just south of Langley. This road led to the shore at Lepe, from which a causeway to the Isle of Wight is supposed to have existed, though this is perhaps just a colourful legend. A more recent local link with history is the fact that Langley Lodge was a childhood home of Lawrence of Arabia. The house no longer exists.

Maps
Landranger 1:50,000
Sheet 196
Pathfinder 1:25,000
Sheets SU 40/50 & SZ 49/59
or Outdoor Leisure Map
Map Reference of Start/Finish
SU447011

How to get there
From Southampton head west along A3024 and A35 to the far end of Totton's southern bypass and turn left there to follow A326, bypassing Marchwood and Hythe to reach Hardley and Holbury, at the far end of which bear right-ahead for Blackfield, through which you continue ahead to adjoining Langley, where The Langley Tavern is on your right. From Bournemouth follow Wessex Way, eastbound A35 and A337 to Lymington, B3054 to Hilltop crossroads a mile beyond Beaulieu, and there bear right to follow the Fawley road. At the next crossroads turn right at traffic lights for Blackfield and Langley, where The Langley Tavern is on your right. Solent Blue Line buses on services 38 and X8 from Southampton and Hythe go on to Langley. Wilts & Dorset buses on services 122, 123 and 124 from Bournemouth connect at Lymington with service 112 to

Beaulieu and Hythe, where connection is made with Solent Blue Line buses on services 38 and X8 from Southampton to Langley.

Pub facilities
Langley Tavern
Built just before World War II on the site of an older hostelry, this combines normal pub amenities with en-suite bed and breakfast accommodation. A good choice of brews including Wadworth 6X, Chiswick Bitter and Boddington's real ales as well as Whitbread Best Bitter and Mild, are complemented by a wide ranging bar menu made possible by recently upgraded kitchen facilities. There are six different kinds of sandwiches, soup of the day, pate and hot toast as well as deep fried mushrooms with garlic mayonnaise, a choice of jumbo jacket potatoes and four different ploughman's. Main meals on offer include scampi or jumbo sausage or chicken portion in a basket, American burger with salad, deep fried cod or plaice fillet with lemon wedge, prime sirloin steak cooked as you like it and served with salad garnish, and gammon steak with fried egg or pineapple, all with chips or choice of potatoes. There is also a vegetarian dish of the day. Apple pie and cream, Black Forest gateau and cream and various ice-creams are available as well as filter coffee On Sundays traditional roasts are lunchtime favourites. The garden includes a children's play area with swings, trampolines, an animal corner and other attractions. Petanque, pool and darts are played. On Sunday evenings

Exbury is a rare surviving example of an estate village still largely populated by estate workers and their families, insulated by woods and water from other centres of population and there is every reason to hope it will so remain: an oasis of peace in a troubled world.

Exbury, it seems, is a corruption of Teocreberie, the name by which the locality was recorded in the Domesday Survey. In times gone by the neighbouring Beaulieu River was sometimes known as the Exe, this being a Celtic term meaning 'the water', though if there is a link, as one might have thought, with the name of Exbury, the placename pundits do not say so.

The village used to be where Lower Exbury now is, a mile from its present location and right at the mouth of the Beaulieu River. The estate was owned by the Mitford family when, in the early 19th century, lord of the manor William Mitford decided to move the village, lock, stock and barrel, to where it is now. New cottages of the local yellow brick were built for his workers. The new church that was also built made use of similar material plus some stonework from the mediaeval chapel at Lower Exbury. Later sheathed in Isle of Wight stone, the modern church contains memorials to members of another landowning family — Lord Forster of Lepe, a 1920s Governor General of Australia, and two of his sons, who died as a result of wounds sustained in World War I.

Lord Forster lived at Inchmery, within yards of the Solent shore. Next on the scene as a major landowner was Lionel Nathan de Rothschild, of the well known banking family, who first bought property locally in 1912. An inheritance in 1916 enabled him to purchase Exbury itself, where after the First World War he set to work to transform 250 acres of tangled woodlands into a rhododendron paradise which has won worldwide renown. Edmund de Rothschild, Lionel's son, now runs the family property, his own son Nicholas also being involved in the care of the famous gardens, which are visited and admired by scores of thousands every year.

The Langley Tavern

there is occasional live entertainment, and Sunday quizzes are popular. Pub-using walkers may use the pub car park, but please ask first. Weekday opening times are 1100-1500 and 1800-2300, with all-day opening in summer, Sunday hours being as usual. Food may be ordered between 1200-1400 and 1800 (1900 Sundays)-2200.

Walk 4

Distance: ***Allow 4 hours for the six-and-a-half mile walk or 5 hours for the eight mile walk.***

Directly north of The Langley Tavern turn left to follow a driveway which becomes a fenced and tree-lined path leading into another road which you follow left-ahead. At a fork of no-through-roads bear left to follow an unadopted road. Beyond bordering houses this becomes a gravelly path which dips between trees to cross by a handrailed footbridge Dark Water brook, itself tree-shaded. The path then rises to pass between oak woodland and pastures margined by trees, soon dipping again before emerging on to a road.

Follow this road right-handed, with a field on your left at first, followed by a wood, just past the start of which you enter it over a stile. A well-defined path now leads you south-westward through oaks and hazels which dip right-handed into a parallel stream valley, while farmland remains visible through trees on your left-hand side. Your path fairly soon joins a track leading to buildings on your right, which you follow ahead, out of the wood, to join a lane which you follow right-handed.

This leads past cottages to a T-junction in Exbury village centre, where you turn right, past the entrance to the estate office on your left. Exbury's Church of St Katharine lies just back from the road, on your right.

If you are energetic, you can extend the six-and-a-half-mile walk to one of about eight miles by continuing north along the road past the second of two lodge cottages on your left, then turning left — not through the wrought-iron gates, which precede a private driveway to Exbury House, but to follow a very narrow metalled lane a few yards farther on. This leads between grassy acres followed by oaks and rhododendrons, passing under an ornate arch between two parts of Exbury Gardens and then descending through more boscage. Dwellings face the lane from your right as you approach the private entrance to a boatyard at Gilbury

Hard. A signposted footpath here turns right to emerge through trees on to the bank of the winding Beaulieu River estuary, a placid waterway best arrived at when high tide is lapping the saltings, with woods and water close together as you look along its course.

Head back the same way to Exbury village, passing the church now on your left (or turn back from it if you omitted the side-excursion to Gilbury Hard) and keep right-ahead at the village centre road junction just beyond. Signposted to Inchmery, the lane you now follow is flanked on your right by parkland and then farmland on both sides. Not very far along it, a footpath sign and a stile on your left precede a path across a field, beyond which the Solent gleams to your right.

You soon enter a wood through which you follow a right-bending ride, the public footpath being waymarked at various subsequent ride turnings. This involves a right-angled turn left to follow a ride which rises to reach the east end of the wood. At a signposted junction of paths here you turn right to follow the wood edge to an opening on your right, through which a grassy strip separates woodland border trees from a conifer plantation. Follow the left edge of the grassy strip, as indicated by yellow waymarks, to a footpath-signposted opening at the end, after passing through which you turn right to follow the wood edge.

Your path next enters the wood once more, continuing parallel with its left-hand edge as far as a grassy right-hand clearing into which the footpath turns, crossing a stream by a plank bridge before rising to leave the wood. Another footpath sign here points your way left-handed along the left edge of a field from which, looking right, you can see Exbury House through a gap in the trees inland.

At this field's far left-hand corner you cross a stile to follow the last few yards of footpath before emerging on to a lane which you follow left-handed for a short distance to the Solent shore at Inchmery. Here a stile with a footpath sign marks the start of a path along the shore which we found under water at high tide. After a pause for lunch we therefore continued along the shore road. Oak trees leaning out over the water precede the grounds of Inchmery House and a junction of lanes where we turned right to follow a signposted fenced path leading through trees back to the shore, along which a gravelly path continues, trending leftward.

On a later visit at low tide I followed the shore path east from Inchmery, picking my way around the debris of cliff erosion at some points but otherwise finding the going quite easy. A myriad oozy crenellations carve up the saltmarsh to the right here, where the Beaulieu River's outflow reaches the Solent after sweeping around Gull Island, part of North Solent National Nature Reserve and a breeding place for large numbers of gulls and other sea birds.

Coast protection work has been carried out alongside the all-states-of-the-tide path which takes you east past Lepe House to where a concrete path leads back on to the road. Follow the road left-handed to where it shortly bends left and at this point cross a stile flanked by a footpath sign on your right. A well-defined grassy farm track leads you right-handed, soon curving left to cross a marshy area before rising to end at a gateway with a broken stile alongside. Cross the large arable field

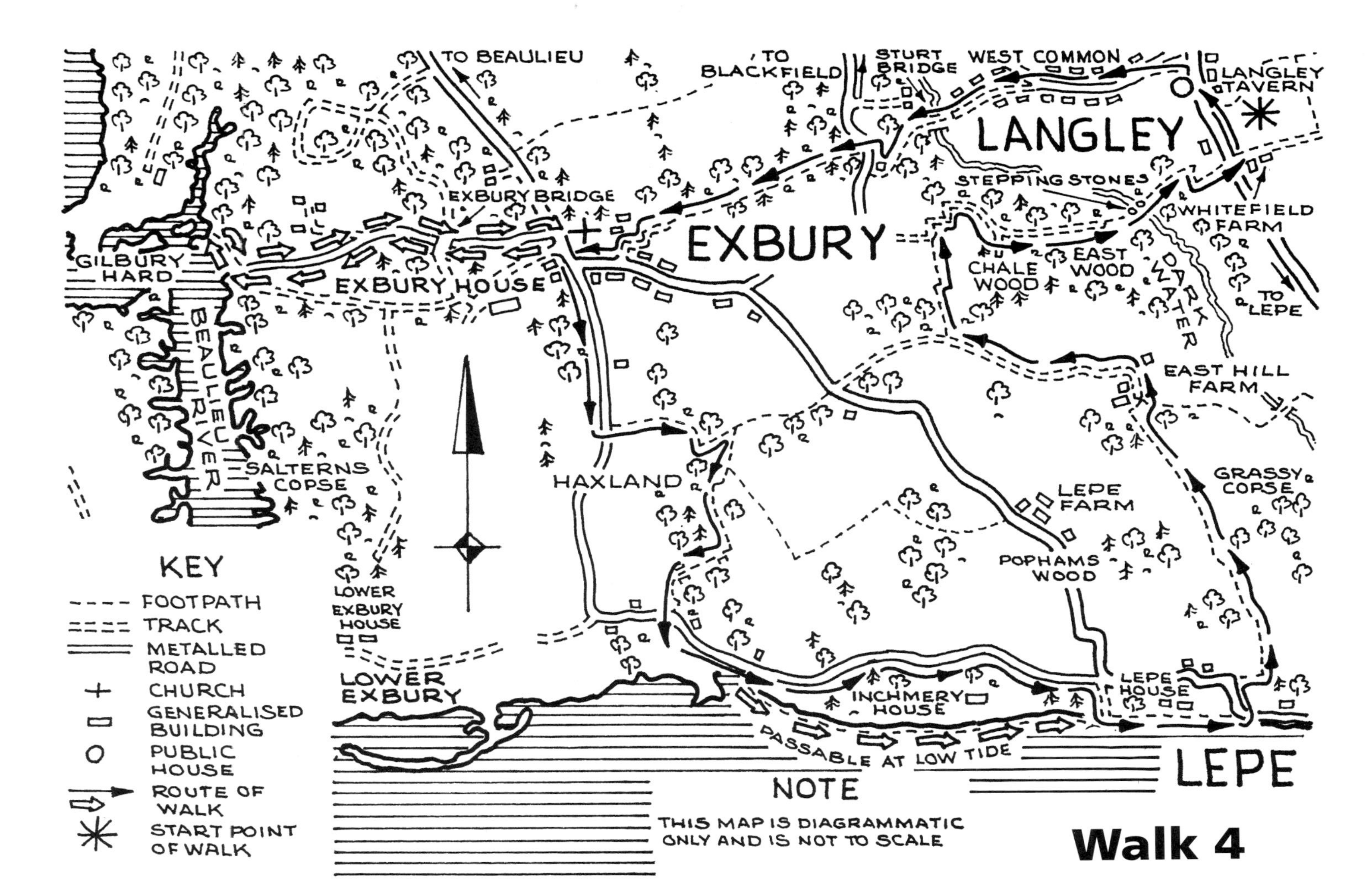
TO BEAULIEU
TO BLACKFIELD
STURT BRIDGE
WEST COMMON
LANGLEY TAVERN
LANGLEY
STEPPING STONES
WHITEFIELD FARM
EXBURY BRIDGE
EXBURY
GILBURY HARD
EXBURY HOUSE
CHALE WOOD
EAST WOOD
DARK WATER
TO LEPE
BEAULIEU RIVER
EAST HILL FARM
SALTERNS COPSE
HAXLAND
GRASSY CORSE
LEPE FARM
POPHAMS WOOD
LOWER EXBURY HOUSE
LOWER EXBURY
INCHMERY HOUSE
LEPE HOUSE
PASSABLE AT LOW TIDE
LEPE
KEY
FOOTPATH
TRACK
METALLED ROAD
CHURCH
GENERALISED BUILDING
PUBLIC HOUSE
ROUTE OF WALK
START POINT OF WALK
NOTE
THIS MAP IS DIAGRAMMATIC ONLY AND IS NOT TO SCALE

Walk 4

Solent shore path at Inchmery

beyond this, heading towards the leftmost corner of the wood on its right-hand side as you look ahead. When you reach this, carry on ahead across the same arable field to a stile preceding a second stile not many yards farther on.

Follow the same footpath alignment across the next large field, heading for a stile alongside a gate on the far side. Take a last look back across farmland to the sea through a frame of trees before following a green ride through the wood that now lies ahead. After crossing a shallow stream you head uphill to skirt right-handed of farm buildings at East Hill Farm, where you join a bridleway which you follow left-handed. A gravelly road now leads you through farmland, with a wood in view to your right.

The wood and the gravel road converge, and where the road-cum-bridleway bends left you pass through a waymarked gateway on your right to follow a woodland ride which angles leftward. At the wood end bear right of another waymarked gate to follow a fenced grassy track, with trees to your right, along the right-hand edge of a field to join a green lane. Follow this grass-centred gravelly lane right-handed along a twisty course into a wood, soon after entering which you disregard a right-turning track as well as subsequent minor tracks and paths diverging to right and left.

A stepped and handrailed path presently descends to concrete block stepping-stones over Dark Water brook, beyond which you climb to follow a gravelly path to a stile and a footbridge which you cross. Leaving the wood, your path angles right to skirt a paddock before bending left to reach the road directly opposite Whitefield Farm, on the Lepe side of Langley. Follow the road left-handed for a few hundred yards to arrive back at The Langley Tavern.

Through Riverside Woods to Bucklers Hard

WALK 5
At least 3 hours
5 miles
Walk begins page 32

Background to the Walk

Beaulieu, so aptly named 'beautiful place', has been a focal point of attraction for outsiders throughout the centuries. Early Norman kings had a hunting lodge here which was known as 'Bellus Locus'. Then, when King John decided to make his peace with the Cistercian monks, he gave them Beaulieu and its surrounding lands for their Abbey of St Mary de Bella Loco Regis.

The abbey, we learn, took 40 years to build and attained a size comparable with that of Winchester Cathedral. The community supported itself by the produce of farms and allied enterprises scattered about an extensive estate stretching down to the Solent. Starting in 1204, the Cistercian era ended when Henry VIII dissolved monastic institutions everywhere and confiscated their lands. Thus in 1538 an ancestor of the present Lord Montagu acquired the property.

The village of Beaulieu probably began as a cluster of cottages built to accommodate the large labour force required to construct the abbey. The original dwellings would have been of mud or wattle-and-daub, the traditional domestic building materials of the area. From the 17th century onwards these were superseded by houses built of locally-made bricks. Many from that period still survive in Beaulieu High Street. Palace House is on part of the site of the old abbey, as is the parish Church of St Mary. Between the abbey remains and the village winds the picturesque Beaulieu River, tidal upstream as far as the bridge. This bridge dates back to the 13th century and was built of quarry-stone by the monks. It made a convenient site for a tide mill which functioned well into the 20th century, having

Maps
Landranger 1:50,000
Sheet 196
Pathfinder 1:25,000
or Outdoor Leisure Map
Map Reference of Start/Finish
SU386022

How to get there
Beaulieu lies at the junction of B3056 from Lyndhurst and B3054 from Lymington and from Dibden Purlieu roundabout, nr Hythe, reached from Southampton via A3024 and A35 to the western end of Totton's southern bypass and from there via A326. At Dibden Purlieu roumdabout take the 5th exit (i.e. turn right) for Beaulieu. Lymington is reached from Bournemouth via A35 to the eastern end of Christchurch bypass and then via A337 by way of Highcliffe and the outskirts of New Milton. Beaulieu can be reached direct from Brockenhurst via B3055 to Hatchet Pond, and then via B3054. The free public car park at Beaulieu lies in the triangle enclosed by B3056, B3054 and Beaulieu High Street. Solent Blue Line services 38, 39, X8 and X9 connect at Hythe or Dibden Purlieu with buses on Wilts & Dorset service 112 to Beaulieu, and on summer Sundays only with buses on

Solent Blue Line service 34, which runs to Beaulieu. Wilts & Dorset bus services 123, 124 and X31 from Bournemouth connect at Lymington with service 112 for Beaulieu, and on summer Sundays Wilts & Dorset service 123 from Bournemouth terminates at Beaulieu instead of Lymington.

Pub facilities
Wine Press, Beaulieu
Open between 1100-2300 on weekdays and between 1200-1500 and 1900-2230 on Sundays, The Wine Press, formerly Spats Bar, is a section of the old-established Montagu Arms Hotel which has been transformed into an attractive pub serving food direct from the hotel kitchen. Decor is imaginatively in keeping with its name, associated as this is with Beaulieu's long tradition of wine-growing, which dates right back to monastic times. Beaulieu medium dry white wine is sold here by the bottle as just one item in a very extensive wine list. Real ales on draught include Old Thumper from Ringwood Brewery, Brakspear and Wadworth 6X. Whitbread Best Bitter as well as draught Guinness and Scrumpy Jack cider. Food may be ordered between 1200-1400 and 1900-2200. The lunchtime menu tempts you with roast of the day and items like lamb and apricot pie with puff pastry, steak and kidney pie cooked in Guinness and individual lasagne to chicken curry on a bed of rice, chilli and rice, beef and mushrooms in a rich wine sauce, scampi and chips,

The Montagu Arms and The Wine Press

been brought back into temporary use during World War II after earlier closure.

The National Motor Museum was founded and developed as a tribute to the marvels of the internal combustion engine by the present Lord Montagu, whose father was one of the pioneers of motoring, having been involved, among much else, with persuading Parliament to allow cars to be driven faster than the once legal limit of 12 mph!

Wheels do not reign unchallenged at Beaulieu. New Forest ponies and donkeys wander at will about the village, though this has not always been the case. Where the Forest proper ends and the Beaulieu Manor estate begins the roads were once gated, and I can just remember a time when these gates were opened by estate staff for every individual car or other item of wheeled traffic, being closed again afterwards to help keep livestock where it belonged, on the open Forest.

Access to alcoholic refreshment has rarely been lacking in this community. The monks made wine from their own vineyards, while the village itself in later years was well supplied with pubs. At one time there were five of these. The sole survivor is The Montagu Arms, so-named since 1742 when what had previously been The George, and before that The Ship, identified itself with the owning family. Today a substantial hotel, this was once a modest village hostelry

Bucklers Hard

barbequed pork and rice, or vegetarian pancake with fresh vegetables. Evening bar snacks include burgers, scampi or jumbo sausage and chips. Children are admitted but the car park is reserved for hotel customers.

Master Builder's House Hotel, Bucklers Hard
This preserves much of the atmosphere of the time when master shipbuilder Henry Adams lived here. Open from 1100-2300 on weekdays and from 1200-1500 and 1900-2230 on Sundays, The Yachtsman's Bar serves real ales including Ind Coope Draught Burton Ale and Tetley Bitter. Also available are John Bull Bitter, Ind Coope Dark Mild, draught Guinness and Strongbow cider. This bar, it has to be said, is somewhat Spartan, with limited seating. Better provided for is The Buffet Bar, next door, serving food between 1200-1400 and between 1900-2100, with a help-yourself service ranging from casseroles, fish and lasagne to soup, salads and ploughman's. Children are admitted to The Yachtsman's Bar, which has beams, an open fireplace and a secluded pub garden.

and the scene of an annual fair dating from 1607. About 100 years ago the first Lord Montagu put an end to this because of drunkenness and riotous behaviour by some who attended.

Bailey's Hard, on the route of this walk, was a local centre for brickmaking and still possesses a Brickyard Cottage. The term 'hard' crops up in several placenames locally and refers to the presence of firm, hard access to salt water over otherwise treacherous mud.

Bucklers Hard is thought to have taken its name from a local family called Buckle. It started life as 'Montagu's Town', the second Duke of Montagu having envisaged it as an English base for the West Indian trade from St. Lucia, his island property. It became, instead, a shipbuilding centre. Between 1698 and 1818 no fewer than 60 vessels were launched here, including a number of men-of-war whose names became famous in England's naval confrontation with Napoleon. The *Agamemnon*, Nelson's favourite, was one of these. New Forest oak was a prime material for building these great ships, and a man who supervised their construction was master builder Henry Adams, whose home is now an hotel. There is a Henry Adams Room where a representation of the great man himself may be seen poring over architectural drawings, while in the Maritime Museum the local world over which he held sway is highlighted for visitors to appreciate.

Bucklers Hard's twin terraces of dwellings flank a scenic descent to the river and look today much as they did when the 'wooden walls' were being erected. The whole village is preserved in such a way that, strolling through it, you feel you are walking back in time to the 18th century, its heyday. While some of the cottages are still lived in, others are presented as time capsules complete with contents just as they were 200 years and more ago — the erstwhile New Inn, the Shipwright's Cottage and a labourer's cottage among them.

Walk 5

Distance: Allow at least 3 hours for this five mile walk.

From Beaulieu's public car park take the pedestrian exit to the High Street, which you cross to follow a signposted gravel footpath between dwellings and around a double bend to a kissing-gate. Back gardens flank your approach to a stile, after crossing which you keep straight on across a paddock to a further stile. Beyond this, you join and follow right-handed a fenced gravel track with a meadow to your left and the wood-bordered Beaulieu River estuary curving away out of sight.

After crossing a cattlegrid flanked by a stile you carry on to where a muddy, tree-bordered creek wriggles in from the river and edges close to the track you are following, which then crosses a strip of woodland — Jarvis Copse. Gravel having ceased at the entrance to a waste water treatment works a little way previously, you emerge from the wood to follow the leftward edge of an arable field, with a line of trees to your left.

This brings you to a gate and stile preceding Bailey's Hard, where Brickyard Cottage, on your left, is a reminder of an industrial activity no longer pursued here. Here your track becomes gravelled again and bends right, being joined from the left by another gravel track before swinging left and budding off the approach route for wheeled traffic to Bailey's Hard, which turns right. By now you are back in woodland, and from this point you follow a straight gravel path south-east for nearly a mile through Keeping Copse, where fenced plantations on your right contrast with older oak woodland between yourself and the river, mostly invisible, on your left.

At the far end of Keeping Copse you join and follow right-handed a gravel road, with meadowland on your right and a muddy estuarine inlet at first on your left, soon followed by Bucklers Hard Yacht Harbour, as the marina here is called. By the marina car park entrance your route angles left to follow a riverside walk and gravel footpath, bringing you soon to the waterside end of Bucklers Hard's one 'village' street.

Margined generously by grass which is flanked in turn by terraced cottages where time looks to have stood still for these last two centuries, the stony street climbs also past the Master Builder's House Hotel, where the Yachtsman's Bar should be open. At the top of the hill, just round the corner on your left, is Bucklers Hard Maritime Museum, the cost of admission to which includes access to what used to be the New Inn, preserved with all its period features as are two adjoining cottage exhibits representing 18th century Bucklers Hard and the home of a labourer of that era. On the other side of the street is the village shop (still

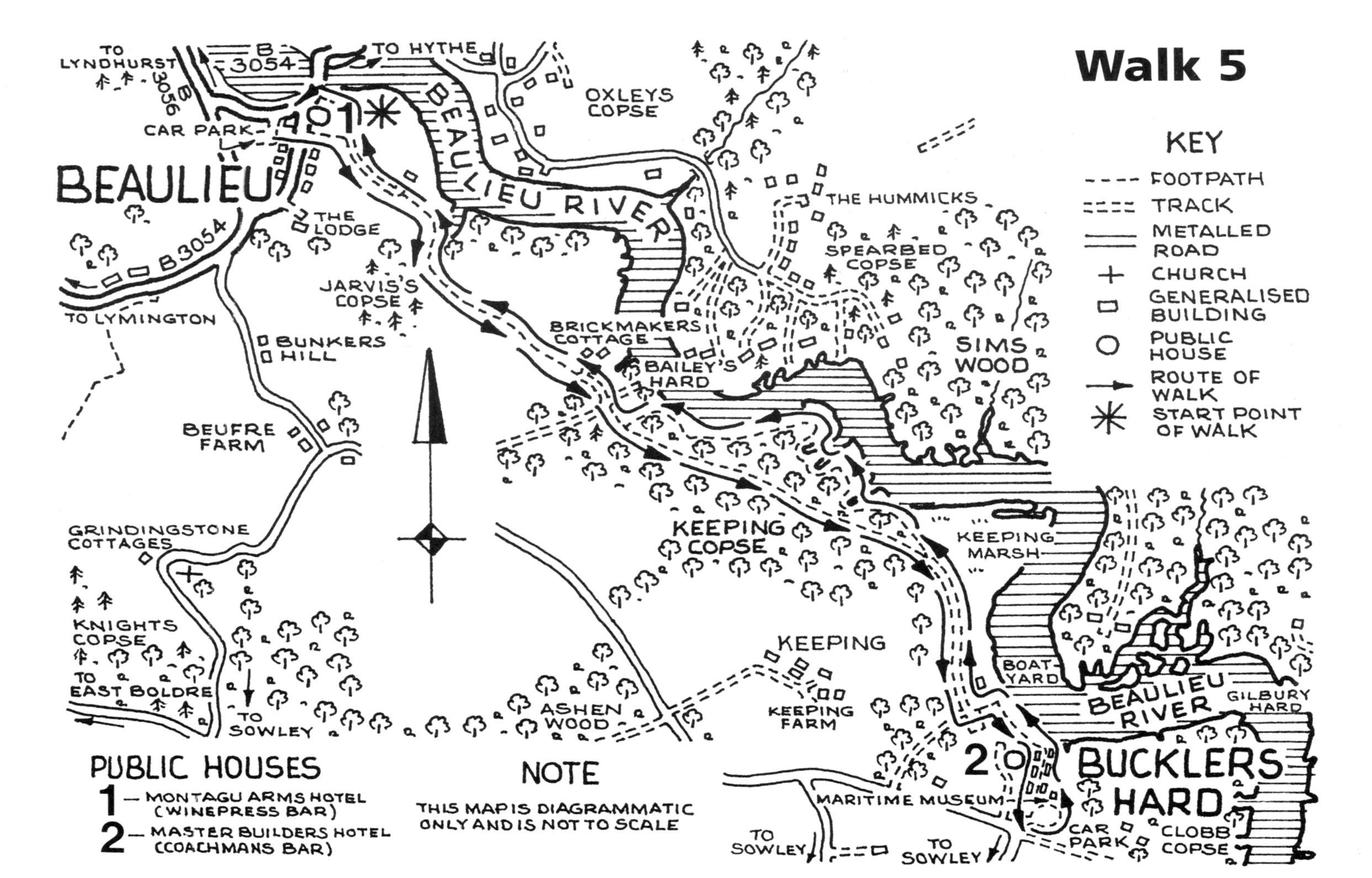

Walk 5
KEY
FOOTPATH
TRACK
METALLED ROAD
CHURCH
GENERALISED BUILDING
PUBLIC HOUSE
ROUTE OF WALK
START POINT OF WALK
TO LYNDHURST
B 3056
B 3054
TO HYTHE
CAR PARK
BEAULIEU
BEAULIEU RIVER
OXLEYS COPSE
THE HUMMICKS
SPEARBED COPSE
THE LODGE
B3054
TO LYMINGTON
JARVIS'S COPSE
BUNKERS HILL
BRICKMAKERS COTTAGE
BAILEY'S HARD
SIMS WOOD
BEUFRE FARM
GRINDINGSTONE COTTAGES
KNIGHTS COPSE
TO EAST BOLDRE
TO SOWLEY
KEEPING COPSE
KEEPING MARSH
KEEPING
KEEPING FARM
ASHEN WOOD
BOAT YARD
GILBURY HARD
BUCKLERS HARD
MARITIME MUSEUM
CAR PARK
CLOBB COPSE
TO SOWLEY
TO SOWLEY
PUBLIC HOUSES
1 — MONTAGU ARMS HOTEL (WINEPRESS BAR)
2 — MASTER BUILDERS HOTEL (COACHMANS BAR)
NOTE
THIS MAP IS DIAGRAMMATIC ONLY AND IS NOT TO SCALE

functioning!) and the shipwright's cottage.

That there is no completely different footpath route making possible a circular walk from Beaulieu does little or nothing to discourage the very large numbers of people who choose to sample at least some of this walk, at holiday time especially. You need not return precisely the same way as you came, though. To begin with, follow the riverside walk and the gravel road to which it leads back past the yacht harbour to Keeping Copse. Entering the wood, fork right from the main gravel path to follow a signposted extension of the earlier riverside walk, a well-defined path which twists and turns in harmony with the serpentine course of the estuary itself, which remains constantly in view through the trees which fringe it, to your right.

The far bank is wooded too, with dense-banked trees punctuated here and there by secluded dwellings of a type and situation which hint at astronomical price-tags and laudatory descriptions in *Country Life*. On your own side trees hem the river without a break for nearly a mile, ensuring many a sheltered corner for waterside wildlife. As well as numerous duck at various points along the tideline, we surprised a solitary curlew.

After many pleasant meanderings, the riverside walk returns you to the more direct gravelled route, which you follow right-handed to Bailey's Hard. The field-edge path beyond this and the fenced track which follows bring you back to the edge of Beaulieu where, instead of recrossing the grassy paddock to reach the High Street and the car park, you can carry on ahead to reach the road right by The Montagu Arms Hotel. Turn left for The Wine Press bar. Not many yards past this, up the High Street, you turn right to re-enter the car park.

A Walk from William Gilpin's Boldre

WALK 6
Allow 3 hours
5 1/4 miles
Walk begins page 37

Background to the Walk

Boldre is a village of the Forest, but not quite in it. The livelihood of those who had their homes here was for centuries linked in various ways with the royal domain on its doorstep. However, not all the means employed by Boldre villagers of the past to help keep body and soul together were calculated to enhance the good of their souls in the Hereafter.

At least, so thought a certain vicar when he arrived in the 1770s to take charge of the local inhabitants' spiritual welfare. The Reverend William Gilpin was appalled by what he saw as the bandit-like habits of Boldre people, much given to poaching and helping themselves to whatever of value they could steal from the wooded wilderness near by. He therefore decided to devote his literary talents to writing books and applying the profits to improving conditions in general for his parishioners. He looked to the Forest for inspiration and found plenty. One of his books in particular, *Remarks on Forest Scenery*, opened the eyes of many to aesthetic rural delights they had hardly noticed until then. It became a classic to rank in importance with a book on natural history by another Hampshire clergyman, the famous Gilbert White of Selborne, at the other end of the county.

Like so many other villages, Boldre today is a quiet place lived in mainly by retired folk and commuters. Yet there is still a sizeable element of those whose links with the soil are not merely ancestral and who could doubtless trace their line back to Gilpin's time.

What is the meaning of the name 'Boldre'? David Mills, in his *Dictionary of English Place-Names*, expresses

Maps
Landranger '1:50,000
Sheet 196
Pathfinder 1:25,000
or Outdoor Leisure Map
Map Reference of Start/Finish
SZ318983

How to get there
The Red Lion at Rope Hill, Boldre is on the south side of the road that heads east through that village from A337 at Battramsley Cross, 2 miles north of Lymington. From Southampton follow A3024 and A35 to Lyndhurst and A337 south from there via Brockenhurst, 3 miles beyond which is Battramsley Cross, where you turn left to follow the road signposted to Boldre and Pilley. From Bournemouth head east along A35 to the eastern end of Christchurch bypass, then follow A337 east via Highcliffe and New Milton's outskirts to Pennington and Lymington, from which you then follow A337 north for 2 miles before turning right at Battramsley Cross for Boldre. Wilts & Dorset buses on service 112 between Hythe, Beaulieu and Lymington pass through Boldre within 100 yards of the pub, and buses on services 56, 56A and 56B between Southampton, Lyndhurst and Lymington,

connecting there with buses on services 121, 122, 123 and 124 from Bournemouth and Christchurch, 118 from Ringwood and New Milton and X31 from Ringwood and Christchurch, pass the turning for Boldre half-a-mile from The Red Lion.

Pub facilities
The Red Lion, Boldre
Open on weekdays from 1100-1500 and 1800-2300 and on Sundays at the usual times, The Red Lion is an Eldridge Pope house serving Hardy Country, Royal Oak and Dorchester Bitter real ales as well as EP Keg Bitter, two draught lagers, Guinness and dry cider. It has two bars, a patio and a beer garden where children are welcome but not dogs. There is a field at the back of the large rear car park where walkers using the pub may leave their cars. Food may be ordered between 1200-1400ish and 1800 (1900 on Sundays) and 2200. The menu typically includes 10 starters, six salads, seven main course dishes, three vegetarian selections, five basket meals, six different ploughman's and 11 varieties of sandwiches as well as various side dishes. Gammon, turkey, salmon, plaice, and chicken Kiev are all featured, along with sweets including such tempting items as sherry trifle with whipped cream and strawberries and cream. For a basket meal you might choose between half a duckling, three lamb cutlets, breadcrumbed scampi, a quarter chicken or three pork sausages. Coffee is served from 10am. Dating from 1680, the building was originally three cottages and a stable and always included an alehouse.

uncertainty as to its origin, but suggests it may be an old name for the Lymington River, on which Boldre lies. This seems likely. Indeed, our old friend D. H. Moutray Read, in his *Highways and Byways in Hampshire*, published in 1908, unequivocally gives Boldre as an alternative name for the river. Support for this conclusion may be gleaned from the fact that the Lymington River, or Highland Water as it is known in its upper reaches, has its source not far from an area called Bolderwood, in the heart of the New Forest, well west of Lyndhurst. Another authority has suggested that the name 'Boldre' derives from a Celtic term meaning 'full stream', which adds further weight to this theory.

Where Boldre ends and Pilley begins would be hard for a stranger to discern without the help of a wayside notice. The name of Boldre's neighbour perhaps derives from the Old English 'pil-leah', meaning 'a wood or clearing where stakes are obtained', or so Mills informs us, not in connection with Pilley in Hampshire but with a northern England namesake.

Walhampton, one might guess, means something like 'home farm by the spring', the Old English for spring (or well) being 'waella'. Walhampton House, now a school, was originally the home of the Burrard family, one of whose more notable members was Admiral Sir Harry Burrard Neale. It was in memory of Sir Harry, who put down the mutiny at the Nore and was

MP for Lymington way back in the days of rotten boroughs, that the Walhampton Monument was raised following his death in 1840. Sir Harry was a friend of William IV, the 'Sailor King', whose widow, Queen Adelaide, was one of several royals who associated themselves with the erection of the monument, a lofty pillar looming beside a lane followed on this walk. It dominates the view as one looks east from Lymington, which various Burrards served as mayors, in Parliament, or in other ways for over 400 years.

Walk 6

Distance: ***Allow 3 hours for this five-and-a-quarter mile walk.***

Immediately east of The Red Lion turn right from the road called Rope Walk to follow Boldre Lane south between trees and houses for nearly half a mile. You then turn left just before the entrance to Shallowmead Nurseries to follow a narrow, sunken, tree-shaded metalled lane. This is signposted as leading to a ford 'unsuitable for motors'. In fact the metalled lane ends abruptly at the bank of the Lymington River, the winding, full-bodied course of which you cross by an iron-railed footbridge.

Where tarmac resumes on the river's far side turn right through a gate to follow a grassy bridleway, heading south with trees to your left and the reed-bordered river, with more trees beyond it, to your right. When cottages and a bridleway sign materialise to your left, climb left between two dwellings, walking round a padlocked metal gate to follow a path joining a concrete road, unfenced on your left, which you follow ahead. Trees on your right screen Vicars Hill, where William Gilpin lived.

Emerging soon past the right-hand entrance to Southlands School, you join School Lane. About ten yards along this, with the entrance to a house called Gilpins right-ahead of you and a large oak in the centre of a grassy triangle to your right, fork left to follow Hundred Lane. At the end of a walled garden on the right-hand side of this, cross a stile adjoining an iron-railed gate on your right. A grass path, dampish in

Beams, inglenook fireplaces and flagstone floors in some bar areas attest its age. Brassware and a large collection of chamberpots decorate the pub interior while windowboxes of flowers add a touch of rural charm outside.

Towle's Restaurant, Walhampton.
Although not a pub as such, this licensed restaurant en route, with its well-appointed bar and internal patio area, makes an ideal halfway house where you can relax over a pint of Royal Oak, Crystal Bitter or Pope's Ale or one of three draught lagers while toying with the bar menu. This is likely to offer items such as half a chicken with vegetables, deep fried scampi or plaice and chips, char-grilled sirloin steak and chips, and poached trout with side salad, not to mention smoked salmon salad with brown bread and a range of other salads as well as ploughman's and various sweets. During the week there is also a full lunchtime and evening a la carte menu. Food orders are taken between 1200-1430 and 1900-2130.

Fleur-de-Lys Inn, Pilley.
With its whitewashed front and eyebrow windows peeping out from under the thatch, this is a picture of old world delight at the heart of a rural Forest community well away from the busier roads. Landlords dating back to AD1498 are listed in the Jacob Armitage bar, which, like the Beverley of Arnwood bar, is named after characters in Captain Marryat's Children of the New Forest. The inn is mentioned in Conan Doyle's

historical novel The White Company. Alcoholic stimulants are said to have been sold here since 1096, only 30 years after the Battle of Hastings, so this may well be the oldest pub in the New Forest. A flagstoned entrance, exposed beams and brickwork emphasise its vintage character, and hams used to be smoked in the chimney above an open fireplace. Brews available include Whitbread Best Bitter, Wadworth 6X, Flower's Original and Symonds Scrumpy Jack cider is on draught. The bar menu lists items ranging from chicken liver pate, prawn open sandwiches, and crab claws with dips and salad garnish to sausage, haddock or breaded scampi with chips, ploughman's, curries, pastas, steaks, chicken dishes, breast of duck in honey and grapefruit sauce with fresh vegetables. Watch the board for daily specials, and there is a good choice of sweets. Lunchtime food may be ordered until 1400 on weekdays and until 1330 on Sundays while evening food orders are taken until 2130 on weekdays and 2100 on Sundays. Pub opening hours are 1100-1430 (until 1400 in winter) and 1800-2230 Mondays to Thursdays and until 2300 Fridays and Saturdays, Sunday opening hours being 1200-1430 and 1900-2230. Well-behaved children are welcome and there are swings for them in the garden. Walkers using the pub may use the pub car park.

places, now leads you south with a wood to your left to join a gravel road which you follow ahead through fenced farmland with views towards Lymington on your right.

This brings you out on to the Beaulieu-Lymington road opposite Walhampton House, the old Burrard family home and now a school. As you follow this road right-handed you pass Towle's Restaurant on your left before turning left to follow winding Monument Lane, one of those placid, tree-lined byways where motor traffic is still sparse enough for walking to be a pleasure. A tree-ringed hump on the right of this supports the Walhampton Monument, a tall stone pillar suggestive of Cleopatra's Needle. Inscriptions on four sides highlight events in the life of Admiral Sir Harry Burrard Neale, the man it was raised to commemorate, and, in the fashion of its period, wax lyrical to the point of excess about his person.

At this point you join The Solent Way, a long distance walking route from Milford-on-Sea to Emsworth which follows the coast wherever it can but is frequently forced to deviate inland and to follow roads instead of paths. The Solent Way leads you on along Monument Lane to where you can glimpse the yacht-studded estuary of the Lymington River, not far ahead and a little to your right.

At the signposted gravel approach to a house called Halyards, on your left, there should also be a Solent Way sign. None was visible when we passed, nor any other indication that the gravel drive is also the first stage of a public footpath. This may well have since been remedied. Anyway, turn left here to the drive's end, where you pass through a wooden wicket gate preceding a tall-hedged path which soon emerges from the trees to follow the left-hand edge of a field. At the end of this you enter a wood to follow a well-defined path leading on ahead. After crossing a stile on your right, the path carries on in the same direction as hitherto, with a fence screening a house on your right and a wood now on your left. The next stile precedes a footbridge over a stream and a muddy patch which can be bypassed to the right before your path rises through woodland to emerge past the remains of a gate on to metalled Snooks Lane.

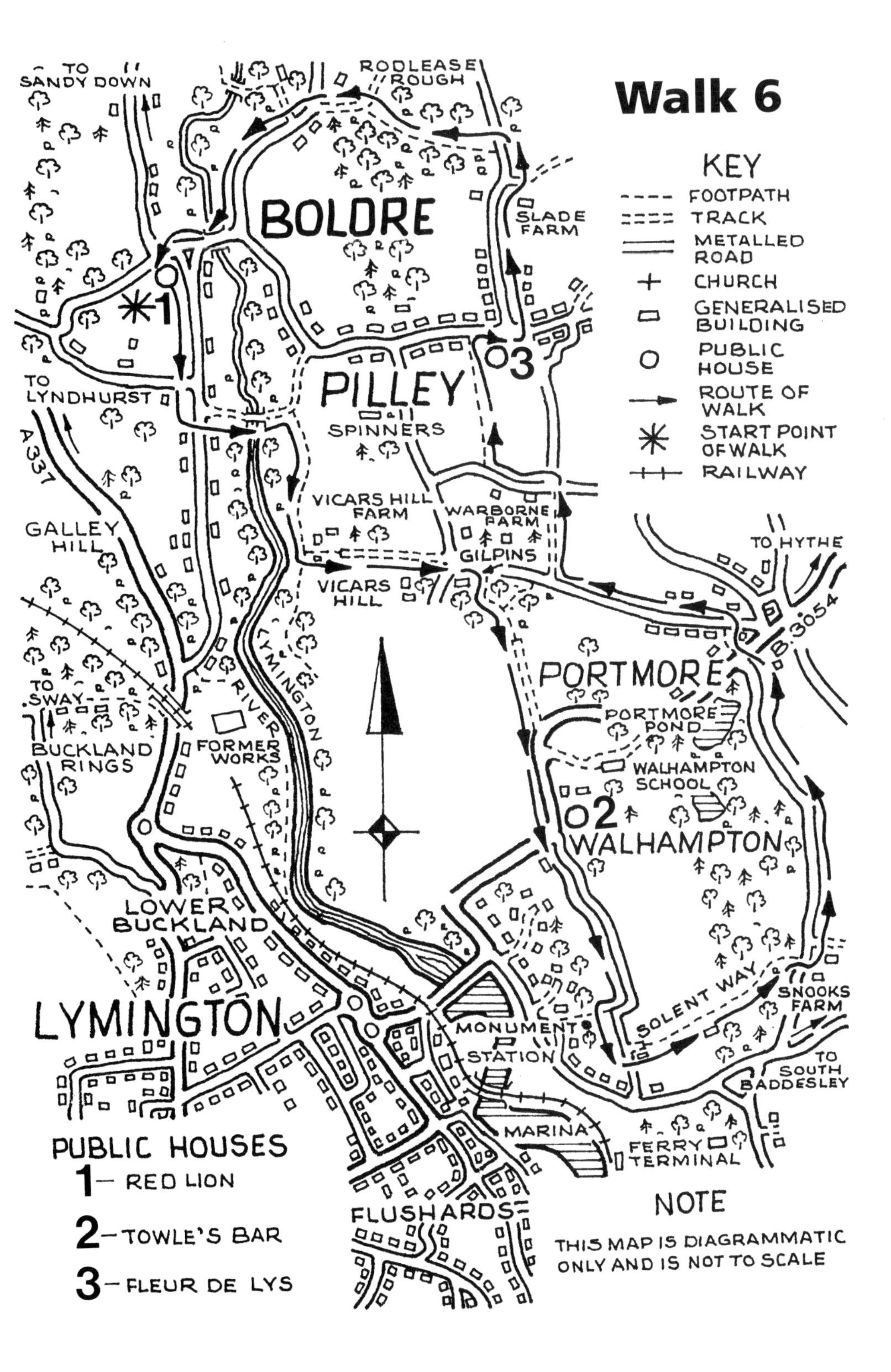

Walk 6
TO SANDY DOWN
RODLEASE ROUGH
BOLORE
SLADE FARM
KEY
FOOTPATH
TRACK
METALLED ROAD
CHURCH
GENERALISED BUILDING
PUBLIC HOUSE
ROUTE OF WALK
START POINT OF WALK
RAILWAY
1
3
2
TO LYNDHURST
PILLEY
SPINNERS
A337
VICARS HILL FARM
WARBORNE FARM
GILPINS
GALLEY HILL
TO HYTHE
VICARS HILL
B3054
LYMINGTON RIVER
PORTMORE
TO SWAY
PORTMORE POND
BUCKLAND RINGS
FORMER WORKS
WALHAMPTON SCHOOL
WALHAMPTON
LOWER BUCKLAND
SOLENT WAY
SNOOKS FARM
LYMINGTON
MONUMENT
STATION
TO SOUTH BADDESLEY
MARINA
FERRY TERMINAL
PUBLIC HOUSES
1 - RED LION
2 - TOWLE'S BAR
3 - FLEUR DE LYS
FLUSHARDS
NOTE
THIS MAP IS DIAGRAMMATIC ONLY AND IS NOT TO SCALE

The Fleur-de-Lys Inn

Encroaching brambles and summer herbage had to be beaten back in places to ease our progress along the footpath just described, and I hope that as part of The Solent Way it may be better maintained in the future. It can be bypassed altogether, if preferred, by following Monument Lane to its end and there turning left. Turn left at the next two lane junctions to join Snooks Lane and follow this north.

Having joined Snooks Lane from the footpath, follow it left-handed, with fields and woodland to your left. This is another quiet byway, very much like Monument Lane and equally pleasant to walk along. Half-a-mile along it, wood-surrounded Portmore Pond can be glimpsed in private grounds to your left a very short distance before you reach the Lymington-Beaulieu road. Cross this, heading slightly right then left to follow a hedged grass path to a stile preceding another road on the western edge of the hamlet of Portmore.

Follow this road left for a few hundred yards, then turn right by a footpath sign to follow a track, hedged on the left and fenced on the right, to reach a short, gated grass section of the track preceding another road, on to which you emerge by Warborne Farm. Follow this latter road left-handed. Where it soon curves left, cross a stile on your right by a footpath sign to follow a path along the right-hand edge of a field. Parkland with scattered trees lies to your left before you pass through a gate on your right and cross a stile to reach Pilley.

Joining a road here, follow it right-handed to pass the old world Fleur-de-Lys Inn on your right. Not many yards beyond the pub turn left to follow Church Lane. Beyond where bordering houses end this crosses a wooded dip, just past the bottom of which a signposted, well used footpath leads you left-handed. Ignore a path which angles left from this and carry on west through a brackeny area just below a wooded slope where tunnelling badgers have their home. Bordering fences flank your approach to a gravel track which you follow left-handed to join a lane. Follow this left-handed in its turn to reach the Pilley-Boldre road, which you follow right-handed across the Lymington River and so back to Boldre, where The Red Lion is on your left about 200 yards ahead.

Coastal Countryside near Pennington at Lymington

WALK 7
Allow 3 hours
4 ½ or 4 miles
Walk begins page 43

Background to the Walk

Pennington was a mediaeval manor and its name is believed to mean 'farmstead paying a penny rent', which certainly does not hint at any great crop-producing potential of the land in this part of Hampshire! Agriculture today is not a major local activity and in centuries gone by the sea was a main source of local employment. From early times until the 19th century extraction of salt from evaporated sea water was carried on at up to 13 salterns on the neighbouring marshes. This only ceased when Cheshire's salt mines were developed as a cheaper source of this commodity. The method employed here was to let sea-water into shallow salt-pans, which would then be sealed off for evaporation to proceed. When this reached a certain point, the resultant brine would be boiled until all that was left was salt.

The Chequers Inn's lonely situation is linked with the saltworks once so close to it. Outgoing consignments of salt were checked here for tax purposes, hence apparently its name, the landlord told me. Working with salt sounds a thirsty business, and The Chequers was well placed to restore body fluids to salt workers on their way home from the day's labours.

With the salterns consigned to history, Pennington Marshes is an important nature reserve to which vast numbers of water-loving birds flock every winter. Migrant species from the Arctic congregate not only on the freshwater marsh but also on the extensive mudflats exposed at low tide. This saltmarsh area has developed on accumulated silt protected against wave action from the open English Channel by the long shingle spit

Maps
Landranger 1:50,000
Sheet 196
Pathfinder 1:25,000
or Outdoor Leisure Map
Map Reference of Start/Finish
SZ322936

How to get there
The Chequers Inn, at Lower Woodside, lies near the end of Ridgeway Lane, a quiet, hedged cul-de-sac forking left from the road that leads south from Pennington Cross, a roundabout (and a Ford garage) on A337 half-a-mile on the Christchurch side of Lymington. From Southampton follow A3024 and A35 to Lyndhurst and A337 south from there via Brockenhurst to skirt Lymington, from which A337 turns west for Pennington Cross. From Bournemouth head east along A35 to the eastern end of Christchurch bypass and then follow A337 via Highcliffe to skirt New Milton and bypass Everton village en route to Pennington Cross, where you turn right. Immediately on leaving the roundabout the lane signposted to Lower Pennington divides, the left-hand one being Ridgeway Lane. Disregard all side turnings from this until you reach The Chequers Inn on

your right, just over half-a-mile ahead. Wilts & Dorset buses on services 56, 56A and 56B from Southampton and Lyndhurst and 112 from Hythe and Beaulieu connect at Lymington with buses on services 121,122,123 and 124 which pass through Pennington en route for New Milton, Christchurch and Bournemouth, and vice-versa, and service 118 to and from Ringwood and New Milton. Limited stop buses on service X31 operate between Lymington, Christchurch and Ringwood.

Pub facilities
Chequers Inn, Lower Woodside
Part of the charm of this pub is its quiet situation along a pleasant rural byway on the seaward side of Pennington, though with the sea still half-a-mile distant. Built about 1670, it has a creeper-covered front and a homely interior. Weekend barbecues are held on the patio, and there is a garden at the back. Brews include Wadworth 6X and Flower's Original as well as two guest ales drawn in the traditional way from hand-pumps. The pub is noted for fish dishes such as grilled lemon sole and trout with prawns and almonds. A typical menu also offers soup, pate or salad starters, Italian pasta, vegetable risotto, roast rack of lamb with a coarse-grained mustard sauce, chicken Wellington, sirloin and rump steaks and mixed grills. Bar snacks include lasagne, chilli, burgers, plaice and chips and scampi. There are facilities for children. Pub-using walkers may use the pub car park and there is

The Chequers Inn, Lower Woodside

at the Solent's western end. The spit forms a pebbly promontory at the end of which looms Hurst Castle, built by Henry VIII as part of his south coast defences against the French and garrisoned until quite recently.

At the landward end of the shingle spit, between it and the outflow of the Avon Water rivulet, is Keyhaven, a yachtsman's paradise. Twelfth century Kihavene was apparently 'a haven where cows were shipped'. Seven centuries later it was the haunt of a certain Colonel Peter Hawker, whose claim to fame was his adeptness at slaughteringwildfowl on Keyhaven's mudflats. The cottage where he lived is still pointed out. Just in case you might miss it, it bears the name-plaque 'Hawker's Cottage', while the pub next door is called The Gun as a further reminder of Hawker's method of exploiting the local wildlife.

The sea wall protecting Keyhaven and Pennington Marshes from inundation by high tides was undergoing extensive repairs when we first tried this walk. Part of the public footpath along it was temporarily closed in consequence, making it necessary for us to use a diversionary path which is probably worth trying as an alternative route anyway, so a description of it is included here. We went back later to try out the coastal route when the work had been completed and the path, a very popular one, was open for use again.

Walk 7

Distance: ***Allow 3 hours for this walk of either four-and-a-half or four miles.***

Having left The Chequers Inn behind you on your right, within yards fork right from Lower Woodside, a southerly extension of Ridgeway Lane, with Chequers Green on your left, to follow a private road which is also the beginning of a public footpath. A few yards along this, at the approach to the private entrance to Pennington House, turn right towards a field entry-point, then almost immediately cross a stile on your left. Follow a fenced path to a stile beyond which you follow the right-hand edge of a meadow for a few yards before crossing another stile, on your right, to follow the left-hand edge of the arable field you now enter. This brings you to yet another stile, after crossing which you continue along the left-hand edge of the next field to a sixth stile preceding Lower Pennington Lane.

Follow this left-handed, past farm buildings, as far as a right-hand metal gate adjoined by a footpath sign. You now follow a path around the gate and along a metalled lane to a gate with a stile alongside it. Roadmetal ends here and a grass-and-gravel track leads on ahead, skirting left of a fairly substantial lake on a former gravel extraction site. Here in winter we saw large numbers of handsome tufted duck, squadrons of coots with their distinctive snowy-white foreheads and, almost inevitably, gulls. Just beyond this man-made nature sanctuary is a metalled lane which you cross. After crossing the stile alongside a further gate directly opposite another grass-and-gravel track leads on ahead across flat ground with pastures on both sides followed by what we found as a refuse infill site on extensive former gravel workings to your left. This ground, a sign informed us, was in the process of being restored for agricultural use. Arable farmland follows and a belt of young conifers and deciduous trees flanks your route on its left-hand side as you approach a gate and stile, beyond which you join a potholed track which you follow right-handed.

This track becomes a minor metalled road after

additional space to park in the road outside. Opening hours are 1100-1430ish and 1800-2300 on weekdays and as usual on Sundays. Food may be ordered between 1200-1400 and 1900-2200 (2130 Sundays).

Gun Inn, Keyhaven

Should you decide to start your walk at this Keyhaven pub instead of at The Chequers you can use the public car park opposite. The pub occupies a 17th century building which in earlier times was a chapel and also a mortuary. Today, despite this history, it is a lively watering-hole for the yachting fraternity, noted for maritime bric-a-brac as well as a large collection of old matchboxes and cigarette cards. Panelled walls enhance its period atmosphere and it has a large garden, a children's room and a patio at the side. Opening hours are 1100-1500 and 1800-2300 on weekdays and as usual on Sundays. Real ales include Ringwood Forty-Niner, Marston's Pedigree and Strong Country, with HSB Bitter and Murphy's Irish stout also on tap. Home made wines are another speciality. Food ordering times are 1200-1430 and 1830 (1900 Sundays)-2130 with a choice of such starters as soup, prawn cocktail, smoked salmon or crab pate followed perhaps by plaice, lemon sole or a quarter roast chicken. Ploughman's, jacket potatoes, garlic-battered chicken goujons, jumbo pork sausages, salads, sandwiches, sweets and ices are also served.

leading you through a gate, not far beyond which you cross a bridge over the outflow of Avon Water. This brings you to Keyhaven, where Hawker's Cottage confronts you to the right of The Gun Inn. At the height of summer this otherwise placid, end-of-the-road backwater is a hive of yachting activity. The winding creek which leads to the open water of the Solent is also traversed by a ferry shuttling to and from Hurst Castle, clearly visible from Keyhaven at the end of a long bank of shingle probing towards the Isle of Wight.

Having sampled what The Gun Inn has to offer, return across Avon Water, directly beyond which the sea wall path to Lymington turns right. Not far along this, on our winter walk, we paused for picnic sandwiches and to watch the first of many migrant brent geese from the Arctic flying to and from their low tide feeding grounds along this shore.

After skirting the yacht-filled channel between Keyhaven and the Solent, the sea wall path steers its way around Keyhaven Marshes, passing gorsey expanses and rough pastureland on your left and bird-thronged mudlands, except when high tide blankets these briefly, on your right. We found the Keyhaven end of the sea wall badly eroded, making it necessary in places to walk along the adjacent shingly strand where the footpath proper had crumbled away. The path re-asserts itself on the sea wall separating a left-hand lake from the sea to your right, with an alternative hard-surfaced track at a lower level to the left of it. About a mile after leaving Keyhaven the path bends sharply right-handed. Repairs to the sea defences resulted in temporary closure of the pedestrian right of way from this point when we first tackled the walk. On our second excursion we were pleased to find that the work had been completed and that the strengthened sea wall and its path were back in service, enabling us to continue our exploration of an area where sea and freshwater marsh bracket an elevated footway affording good views across the spreading watery wilderness on both sides.

Bring binoculars and a bird-recognition guide to make the most of opportunities to identify a host of species which make this wet world their home. Low tide brings wading birds in their multitudes to probe for food in the tidal ooze. Watch out at all times for oystercatchers, redshank, curlew, herons and, on the creeks and marshland pools, smart-plumaged shelduck, one of our largest wild duck species. If you walk this way in autumn or winter many other seasonal visitors, ranging from dunlin to black-tailed godwits, red-breasted merganser, eider duck and large flocks of brent geese from the Arctic, as already mentioned, may be expected. Birds we saw when we walked here in winter ranged from sparrow-sized rock pipits to a solitary short-eared owl hunting the freshwater marsh in daylight — this last was a pleasing sight indeed of a species scarce in southern England.

Another particular pleasure of a walk along this wall between Pennington Marshes and salt water is the marked contrast between the level terrain and seascape close at hand and the looming contours of the land across the water, some three miles distant. The Isle of Wight, where woods and downlands rear beyond the Solent seaway, has an intimacy here with the mainland which results from its

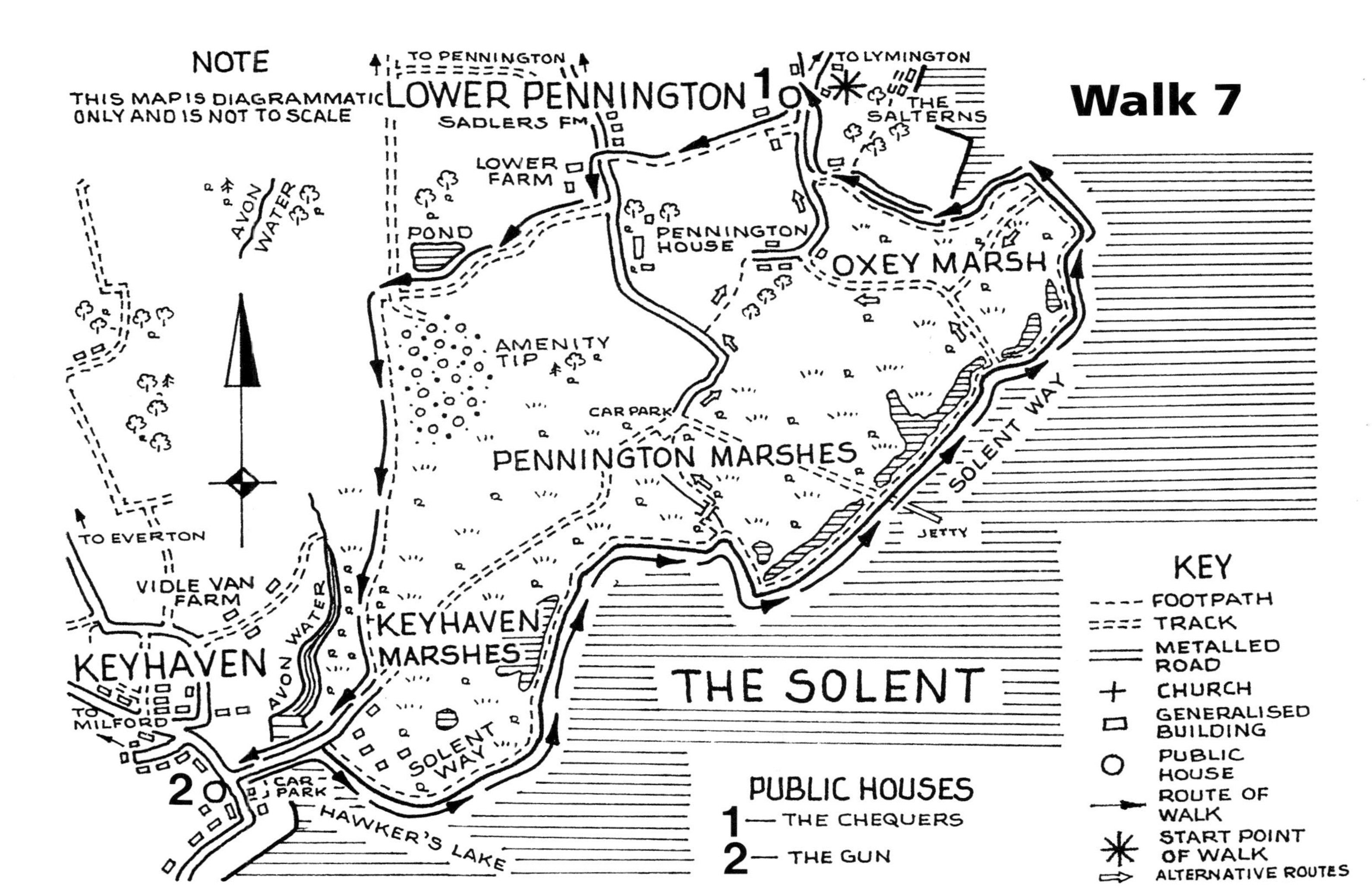
Walk 7
NOTE
THIS MAP IS DIAGRAMMATIC ONLY AND IS NOT TO SCALE
TO PENNINGTON
LOWER PENNINGTON
1
TO LYMINGTON
THE SALTERNS
SADLERS FM
LOWER FARM
AVON WATER
POND
PENNINGTON HOUSE
OXEY MARSH
AMENITY TIP
CAR PARK
PENNINGTON MARSHES
SOLENT WAY
JETTY
TO EVERTON
VIDLE VAN FARM
AVON WATER
KEYHAVEN MARSHES
KEYHAVEN
THE SOLENT
TO MILFORD
2
CAR PARK
SOLENT WAY
HAWKER'S LAKE
PUBLIC HOUSES
1— THE CHEQUERS
2— THE GUN
KEY
FOOTPATH
TRACK
METALLED ROAD
CHURCH
GENERALISED BUILDING
PUBLIC HOUSE
ROUTE OF WALK
START POINT OF WALK
ALTERNATIVE ROUTES

The Gun Inn, Keyhaven

being closer than at any other point, presenting a picture of exceptionally quiet, come-hither enchantment.

Within two miles the sea wall path bends left alongside a narrow inlet, across the upper reaches of which it turns right but where you descend some steps to keep straight on to the head of the creek. Here your path turns left, parallel with a driveway to a house, to join and follow an oak-bordered lane which leads right-handed, bringing you back to The Chequers Inn 200 yards or so along it.

The route back to this which we followed 'first time round' makes use of a track which turns left at the point where the coastal path bends right after passing through the swing-gate a mile after leaving Keyhaven. What looked like a temporary bridge, but which has been left in place as part of an alternative route for walkers, if you decide to opt for it will take you over a marshland waterway preceding a track along the leftward edge of an area of flat grassland, with a deep-set channel of water flanking the wetland to your left. This brings you to a road preceded and followed by swing-gates, beyond the second of which you join and follow ahead a narrow metalled lane. A little way past where this soon bends left you follow a fenced gravel path turning right. After skirting right of a tree-surrounded pond favoured by swansthis path becomes a track leading to a gate preceding the stub-end of a metalled lane which you follow ahead. Not far along this lane, on your left, is The Chequers Inn and your walk's end. Should you decide to shorten the coastal section of this walk by heading back to your car by this inland route, total mileage will be four, not four-and-a-half.

Another alternative conclusion is to continue along the strengthened sea wall and the gravel path which surmounts it for a limited distance before taking either the first or the second gravel track diverging left. Each of these leads through a gateway and then across the flat marshland— Oxey Marsh — that spreads beyond. The two tracks fairly soon unite to follow a common course to a gate, beyond which you follow the right-hand edge of rough pastureland to a stile. A few yards beyond this you join and follow right-handed the metalled lane that soon brings you back to The Chequers Inn at Lower Woodside.

Streamside and Shore near Milford-on-Sea

WALK 8
Up to 4 hours
6 miles
Walk begins page 49

Background to the Walk

Hampshire's Downton is a very small place on the notoriously twisty stretch of A337 that runs between Everton and New Milton, bypassing Milford-on-Sea and the coast. You could almost be forgiven for passing through it in a hurry and hardly noticing that it exists. Lacking a church, it has for its focal point the Royal Oak pub, right on the crossroads at its centre. The pub has been there for 300 years and the oak which shades part of its front may well be as old, though not perhaps royal. The name Downton, experts tell us, means 'farmstead on or by the hill or down' and indeed farmland still surrounds Downton. Of hill or down there is no sign, although it has to be borne in mind that the term 'down', as used in Hampshire, is not exclusive to the county's chalk hill areas — as witness Emery Down, near Lyndhurst, and Browndown, near Gosport.

Delving into the past, we find that 13th century Downton was recorded as 'Duneketon'. This became 'Donketon' the following century, which firmed up as 'Donckton' between the 16th and 18th centuries, then to become 'Dounckton' or, as some would have it, 'Dunkerton'. Whatever the origin of 'our' Downton, it appears to have first come to notice during the reign of Henry III as the property of the heirs of one Elizabeth de Granges, who held it as lessees, in effect, of the lord of the manor of Christchurch.

Between Downton and the coast, just a mile away to the south-west, is a tract of unspoilt countryside the survival of which, in these parts, must be counted almost as a miracle. This makes the initial approach to the gravelly cliff overlooking Christchurch Bay a very

Maps
Landranger 1:50,000
Sheets 195 and 196
Pathfinder 1:25,000
or Outdoor Leisure Map
Map Reference of Start/Finish
SZ269934

How to get there
Not to be confused with Downton in Wiltshire's Avon Valley, the Downton where this walk starts is in Hampshire on A337, the Christchurch-Lymington road, 2 miles east of New Milton. From Southampton follow A3024 and A35 to Lyndhurst and A337 from there via Brockenhurst, Lymington and Pennington. Alternatively, follow A3024 and A35 to the western end of Totton bypass, A326 from there to Dibden Purlieu, B3054 from there via Beaulieu to Lymington and from there follow A337 via Pennington to Downton. From Bournemouth follow A35 to the eastern end of Christchurch bypass and from there follow A337 east via Highcliffe and the outskirts of New Milton. Bus access from Southampton is via Wilts & Dorset services 56, 56A or 56B to Lymington and service 123, 124 or X31 from there to Milford-on-Sea, starting there instead of at Downton.

Milford-on-Sea may be reached from Bournemouth by Wilts & Dorset bus services 123 or 124 and from Ringwood and Christchurch by service X31. Occasional buses on service 123 pass through Downton.

Pub facilities
Royal Oak, Downton
Established in AD1695, this quiet country pub was extended in 1713 and has been run by the same family for over 130 years. Opening times are 1100-1430 and 1800-2300 on weekdays and 1200-1430 and 1900-2230 on Sundays. Brews include Whitbread Best Bitter, Wadworth 6X, Brakspear Bitter and draught Guinness. Food may be ordered between 1200-1400 and 1830-2130 (1900-2100 on Sundays) and is served in a peaceful atmosphere with no jukebox or bar games. There are separate bars for smokers and non-smokers. Home-cooked dishes include soup and daily specials (such as seafood pie with new potatoes), with traditional roasts on Sundays. Regular items include a choice of 5 starters, 5 main courses, 3 vegetarian courses, 9 'lighter bites'as well as 5 sweets and a hot sweet of the day. A typical meal might start with garlic bread and cheese, garlic mushrooms or home made pate, followed by steak pie, fisherman's hot pot, haddock lasagne, grilled fresh trout and almonds or chicken curry and rice. Vegetarians might opt for broccoli mornay or country pancake and jacket potato. Children under 14 are not allowed in the bars but the garden includes a grassed

The Royal Oak at Downton

pleasant cross-country walk with an equally pleasing culmination: a stretch of shoreline viewed from a footpath high enough above sea-level to present a panorama extending from Dorset in the west to the Isle of Wight in the south-east.

Modern Milford is very different. Delightful enough is the triangular village green, but among its flanking shops and cottages there are not many which pre-date development of the one-time sleepy village into a coastal retirement haven. This was instigated in 1887 by landowner Colonel William Cornwallis-West, its more outstanding elements being a string of seaside dwellings of a size and type appropriate to the time when they were built. Before this happened, Milford-on-Sea was just Milford. The mill must have been on Danes Stream, a substantial brook whose bosky meanderings gladden the homeward stretch of this walk for those who set out from Downton, or its outset stage for walkers starting at Milford. This stream reaches the sea via Sturt Pond, a brackish lake which fills with salt water when incoming tides from the Solent reverse the flow of the brook's seaward section.

Jutting out for a mile between the Solent and the open Channel is Hurst Beach, a shingle spit created by tidal action over the ages and nowadays reinforced artificially to keep it in being as a barrier against rough seas flooding in to erode low-lying land on its sheltered side. At the end of the spit, and nearer the Isle of Wight than the Hampshire mainland, is Henry VIII's Hurst Castle, important for coastal defence until well within living memory. Nowadays maintained as an ancient monument, it is accessible either on foot along the length of the shingle spit or, in the summer season, by ferry from Keyhaven, just east of Milford.

Not only was Milford not always known as Milford-on-Sea, but until about the year 1800 it was an inland parish separated from direct contact with the coast by a strip of land belonging to the parish of Hordle. This was worn away by wind and water action during the course of the 19th century, leaving Hurst Spit and its castle as an isolated fragment attached to Hordle rather than Milford. Today, for local government purposes, both are part of the borough of Lymington.

Milford's All Saints Church is a successor to one on the same site which was recorded in Domesday Book. One of only two in the New Forest area to be thus featured, the other being at Brockenhurst, the church at Milford at the time of the Norman Conquest was almost certainly a wooden structure. This was replaced by a Norman church of stone, the foundations and southern arcade of which are embodied in the present typically Early English building, a product of the 13th century. The tower is of this period, an earlier one having blown down during the reign of King John.

children's play area with swings and slides. Walkers using the pub may leave their cars in the large rear car park.

Smugglers Inn, Milford-on-Sea
Open all day on weekdays from 1030-2300 (until 2330 Fridays and Saturdays) and as usual on Sundays, this village pub with its low beamed ceilings dates from 1803 and was originally The Crown. Public car parks adjacent. Wadworth 6X, Strong Country and a guest real ale are on draught as well as Whitbread Best, Guinness and Murphy's and Strongbow cider. Live music most evenings including jazz every Monday and in the large garden there are swings, slides and a children's 'smuggling boat'. The food menu includes a good choice of starters and main courses, daily specials including a roast of the day and a daily three-course lunch as well as basket meals, ploughman's, salads and vegetarian dishes. Specials include strips of beef in fresh ginger and soya sauce, chicken Provencale, steak and kidney pie, seafood crepes, home-made chilli, curry, sweet and sour pork and lasagne with salad. A good choice of sweets available.

Walk 8

Distance: ***Allow 4 hours for this six mile walk.***
Follow for a few hundred yards the twisty, tree-bordered lane which heads south from Downton cross-roads. Watch out for a right-hand metal gate flanked by a double-stepped wooden stile, which you cross. Signposted 'Public footpath to the sea', the grass-centred gravel lane you now follow is fenced on your left and hedged at first on your right, with fields on both sides. Where the right-hand hedge and fence soon end, continue ahead along a field-edge path to the near side of a wooded gully. Here you turn left to cross a metal-barred, stepless stile and follow a fenced path south, with the wood to your right. Summertime herbage is apt to encroach here, but we were pleased to find it had been trimmed back for walkers.

At the wood end cross a second metal stile, where a waymarking arrow keeps you on course as you keep straight on at first, with a fence and field to your left and scattered trees in a valley pasture to your right. Your path soon veers right-handed to cross the grassy valley, where a concrete bridge preceded and followed by stepless double-barred stiles takes you across Danes Stream. Follow the left-hand meadow-edge fence uphill to a double metal-barred stile where a footpath sign directs you slightly right-handed.

Here you reach the Milford-New Milton road, a few yards along which, on its far side as you head right, is Taddiford car park. A double-fenced gravel path leads from this between pastures to the clifftop, on our way towards which a migrant wheatear flashed its brilliant white rump as it flew out from one of the fence-posts. This was towards the end of summer, a time of year when birds of this species are preparing to depart to warmer latitudes for the winter and bracing themselves for a cross-Channel flight as the first stage of their southerly journey.

On the day of our walk the clifftop overlooked a placid bay where the rhythmic swish of waves against shingle was the only sound apparent. We made our way down the broken cliff-face to sit on a concrete slab close to the tideline and watch the patrolling flight of terns, those so-called sea-swallows which look superficially like gulls but are so much more graceful.

These cliffs of gravel and clay are badly subject to erosion — not so much from the sea itself, which has the pebble beach against which to vent most of its wrath, but from wind and rain beating against them as tempests sweep in from the Channel.

Regaining the clifftop, if you have enjoyed a brief break on the water's edge, follow the coast path eastwards, with fields to your left and the cliff to your right. Part-gravel and part-clay surfaced, the path becomes tarred and gravelled as you head east past Hordle Cliff, a popular bathing spot where the beach may be reached by steps from a public car park. Wayside seats become a feature as road and clifftop almost converge at the western end of Milford-on-Sea. The tar-and-gravel path ends where you reach and skirt a boarded-up concrete building to continue along a flagstoned path, with beach huts now to your right, the cliff having ended.

The path becomes shingly as you approach and pass Marine Cafe, with its car park, beyond which a shingle bank to your right at the beginning of Hurst Spit flanks your approach to a robust footbridge where you cross Danes Stream at its outflow from Sturt Pond. As already noted, rising tides convert this to an inflow, flooding Sturt Pond with salt water.

With your back to the sea, you now head left along a path of gravel and flint, with Sturt Pond to your left and a caravan park to your right. Streamside reeds and maritime pines precede the point where a stepped path joins a metalled cul-de-sac which you follow left-ahead, with dwellings to your right. Within a very short distance you once again follow a brookside path from a point where The Solent Way's blue arrow logo identifies the route as part of the long distance coastal walk of this name from Milford-on-Sea to Emsworth.

Another stout footbridge soon takes you back over the fish-haunted Danes

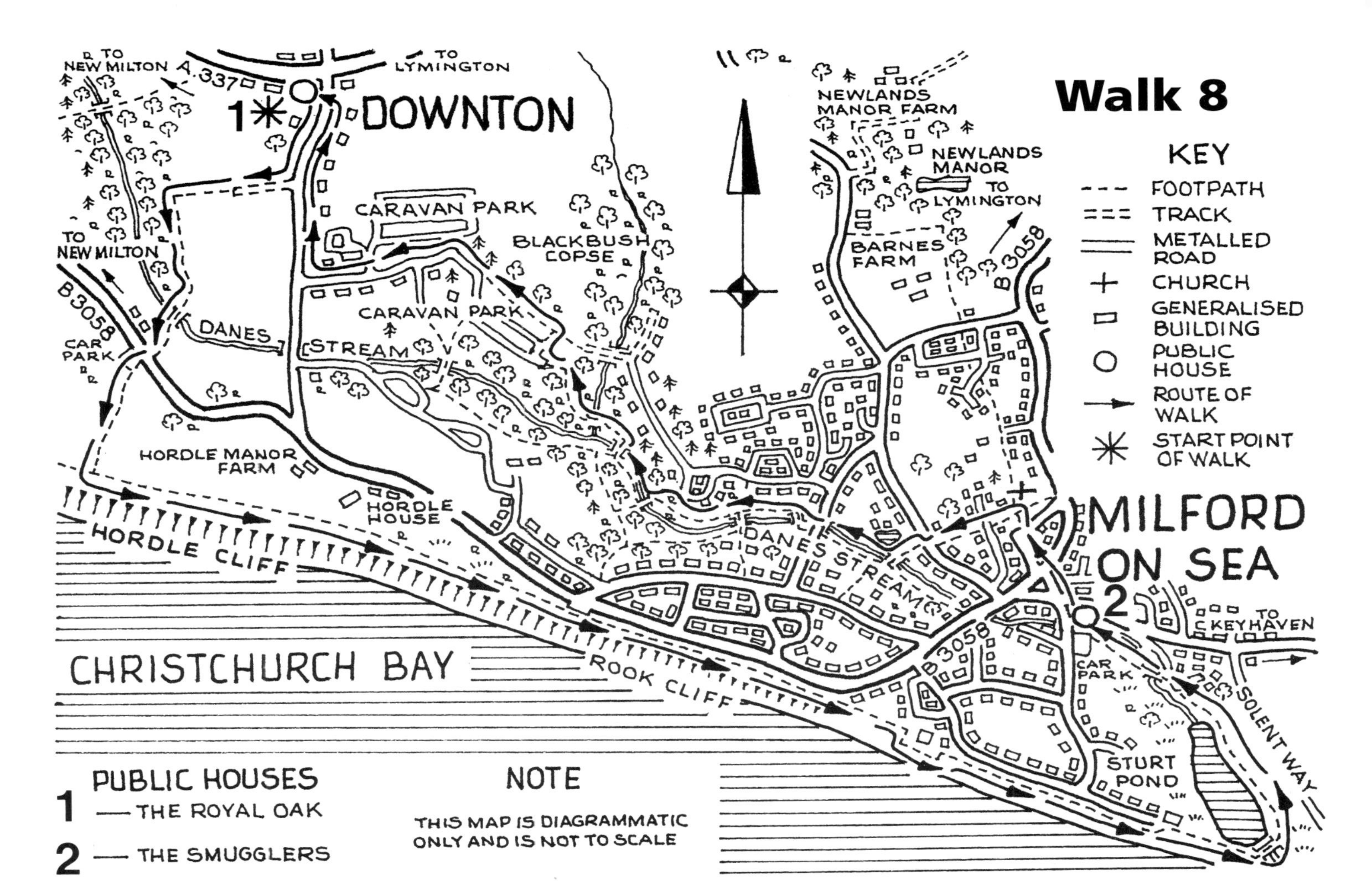
Walk 8
KEY
FOOTPATH
TRACK
METALLED ROAD
CHURCH
GENERALISED BUILDING
PUBLIC HOUSE
ROUTE OF WALK
START POINT OF WALK
TO NEW MILTON
A.337
TO LYMINGTON
1
DOWNTON
CARAVAN PARK
BLACKBUSH COPSE
NEWLANDS MANOR FARM
NEWLANDS MANOR
TO LYMINGTON
BARNES FARM
B 3058
TO NEW MILTON
B 3058
CAR PARK
DANES
STREAM
CARAVAN PARK
HORDLE MANOR FARM
HORDLE HOUSE
HORDLE CLIFF
DANES STREAM
MILFORD ON SEA
2
TO KEYHAVEN
B 3058
CAR PARK
STURT POND
SOLENT WAY
CHRISTCHURCH BAY
ROOK CLIFF
PUBLIC HOUSES
1 — THE ROYAL OAK
2 — THE SMUGGLERS
NOTE
THIS MAP IS DIAGRAMMATIC ONLY AND IS NOT TO SCALE

Stream to emerge by way of a car park, adjoining which are public conveniences. This brings you out on to a road which you follow right-handed to cross Danes Stream again. You then skirt right of Milford's village green, with The Smugglers to your right as you approach the main village road, which you cross straight over to follow a road called Church Hill.

The church is at the top of this incline, where there has been a place of worship for perhaps 1,000 years. Spare time to look around All Saints: spacious and dignified is how the church was summed up in that monumental work of reference, the *Victoria County History of Hampshire*, published before the First World War, and it is certainly both of these things despite its modest size.

With the church to your right after you have left it, follow a churchyard path as far as a lamp-post and there turn left to leave the churchyard by way of a metal kissing-gate. This precedes a hedge-bowered sunken footway very suitably called Love Lane, which leads to a metalled road called The Orchard. Cross this and follow the path which continues ahead to the next road, which you follow right-handed past the first house which confronts you when you reach it. You then turn left to follow a hedged path to a concrete bridge over a stream, beyond which a pond overlooked by houses lies to your right.

Directly ahead is our old friend the Danes Stream, winding its way through a woody valley whose course you follow for some distance after crossing a metal footbridge and then turning right at a footpath T-junction. Sycamores shade your gravelled footway, with Danes Stream between you and houses to your right. Cross the next road and then bridge the stream once more. Ignore a right-turning path and keep right-ahead at the next path junction, disregarding a path which diverges left to bridge the stream in its own turn.

At the next T-junction of paths turn left to bridge the stream yourself and then turn right to follow the valley, ignoring a path which bears left-handed. You next cross Danes Stream yet again and a subsequent tributary brook before following a fenced path which climbs right-handed into a holiday caravan park. If route directions from Love Lane up to here seem slightly confusing, the important thing to remember is to disregard all paths that lead away from the stream valley until you have no option but to enter the caravan park. Here you turn right at a service road junction within the park to climb to the upper edge of the site, where from a T-junction of paths you follow a fenced and hedged path left-handed.

This joins a metalled road which you follow right-ahead past the caravan park. At first confined to ground on your left, this later spills over to your right, where you pass the clubhouse of what announces itself as Shorefield Country Park. If the name 'Shorefield' sounds as though it may have been dreamed up to sound seductive to intending holiday caravanners, in fact it is thoroughly un-phoney, dating from at least the 16th century. Shorefield Road leads on ahead to a T-junction of roads where you turn right for the final half-mile of your walk, back to The Royal Oak at Downton.

Footpaths and Forest Tracks near Tiptoe

WALK 9
Allow 4 hours
$7\frac{1}{2}$ miles
Walk begins page 55

Maps
Landranger 1:50,000
Sheet 195
Pathfinder 1:25,000
or Outdoor Leisure Map
Map Reference of Start/Finish
SZ257971

How to get there
From Southampton follow A3024 and then A35 west via Totton's southern bypass, then via Ashurst, around Lyndhurst and across the New Forest to Holmsley, at the far end of which turn left to follow B3058 for nearly 3 miles to where it crosses B3055 a mile north of New Milton. Now follow B3055 left for a mile to reach The Plough Inn on your left. From Bournemouth follow Wessex Way and A35 east around Christchurch and then north-east to a point half-a-mile beyond The Cat & Fiddle Inn at Hinton Admiral. Here turn right to follow B3055 for 3 miles to reach The Plough Inn on your left. Frequent trains between Southampton and Bournemouth stop at New Milton, from which Wilts & Dorset buses on service 193 to Bashley and Tiptoe pass The Plough Inn.

Background to the Walk

The New Forest's southern borderland is peppered with villages and hamlets which have grown in size and have sometimes coalesced as population has increased during the course of the 20th century. Tiptoe, between Sway and New Milton, is fairly typical of these places. Now quite a populous community, it began life as an insignificant appendage of the substantial parish of Hordle, stretching from the Forest itself to the coast beyond Milford-on-Sea. Although now somewhat overshadowed by some of its faster-growing neighbours, Hordle in the past was a place whose importance matched its size. The Domesday Survey recorded it in AD1086 as 'Herdel'. Two centuries later this became 'Hordhill', which is closer to the name's original meaning, supposedly signifying a hill where treasure had been found.

Wootton, a mile west of Tiptoe, is not so much a village or even a hamlet as a scattering of dwellings which have sprung up at various times along the edge of the Forest proper. The placename Wootton is a common one meaning 'farmstead in or near a wood', which is as appropriate for this area today as it ever was. While nearby New Milton has grown from virtually nothing into a town in the course of a century, Wootton, just north of it, remains unsophisticatedly rustic, a home for people who love the countryside and especially for those who enjoy spending leisure time with horses.

The local farmland, if it may strictly be so described now, is given over almost entirely to providing pasturage for horses. Pony paddocks keep you company as

Pub facilities
Plough Inn, Tiptoe
Open all day from 1100-2300 on weekdays and at the usual hours on Sundays, this Whitbread Wayside Inn serves food from 1200-1400 and 1900-2200. Dating from 1630 and thought originally to have been a farmhouse, the pub has cob walls and interior panelling which go far to preserve its period atmosphere, while hanging flower baskets by the front entrance underline its country character. Families are well catered for, with no restriction on children except in the bar area. Garden includes a children's play area with slides and amusements. Two open fires in cold weather. Real ales available include Winter Royal, Brakspear, Boddington's, Wadworth 6X and Flower's Original. Home cooked food highlights country pies among a good choice of bar snacks including five different ploughman's. The summer menu lists 3 starters, 3 fish dishes and 5 main meals ranging from hearty grills and roast chicken to sausage, mash and beans, and lasagne. Special dishes for children. Dogs no problem, and pub-using walkers may leave their cars in the car park.

The Rising Sun, Wootton
This Forest-edge Whitbread pub was due for refurbishment when this book went to press. It is likely to re-emerge as an all-day pub with a full restaurant licence and with meals at any time of the day, weekdays and Sundays.

The Plough Inn, Tiptoe

you follow the paths and byways of the earlier and later parts of this walk. On the route's middle section, within the Forest, many of the folk you will meet are likely to be local riders, exercising steeds whose home pastures are in the Tiptoe or Wootton areas.

The equestrian link is reinforced by repeated sightings of forest ponies, not only on the open heathland but in the timber inclosures theoretically fenced against these animals. Time was when New Forest commoners' animals and plantations of growing trees were kept fairly rigidly apart, for the good of the trees. Some of those entitled to exercise common rights, however, were not above being tempted to open a gate and allow their stock to enter the woods with all the lush grazing to be enjoyed there. Today they hardly need to bother — the ponies find their way in anyway, and once inside they tend to remain. Some years ago a chief forester, now retired, told me he reckoned there were more ponies in the 'forbidden' inclosures than out of them. On another occasion I was told by the New Forest's Deputy Surveyor of the time, that one of his aims while in office was to clear all the ponies out of the inclosures and keep them out.

That he did not manage to achieve this is bad news for rare butterflies and other wildlife dependent upon a rich and varied flora such as the fenced woods can only produce in the absence of heavy grazing pressure. This fact is recognised by English Nature and by other bodies concerned with advising on habitat conservation, but until some practical means of rectifying the problem is discovered the situation is unlikely to change.

As it happens, we saw ponies in only one of the two inclosures on this walk — Set Thorns Inclosure. In the other inclosure, Wootton Copse, instead of ponies we saw four fallow deer as the highlight of our outing. This may have had to do with the fact that Wootton Copse attracts fewer strollers from nearby populated areas to disturb these shy forest denizens, used as they are to a modest degree of incursion by dog-walking humans.

Until the middle 1960s these two forestry inclosures, in common with Broadley, Brownhill and Holmsley Inclosures, were separated by a railway from the more central parts of the Forest. The original Southampton-Dorchester railway, the line in question, was then closed, and part of its route east of Holmsley station was converted into a road. While the railway was still in service it was something of a barrier to free movement by New Forest fallow deer, although I do recall seeing this species in Set Thorns Inclosure on one occasion when trains were still in operation. Now the railway is no more there is no such hindrance to deer movement, yet fallow are still not over-plentiful at this south-western end of the Forest. There are, however, some roe deer, and the odd muntjac — a miniature Asiatic deer species introduced to Britain almost a century ago — has reportedly been sighted.

Walk 9

Distance: Allow 4 hours for this seven-and-a-half mile walk.
From The Plough Inn, at the westernmost extremity of Tiptoe, head west for about one-third of a mile along B3055, a busy road with discontinuous grass verges along which you need to walk with care. After crossing the wooded valley of the Danes Stream, a substantial brook which winds south-east to meet salt water near Milford-on-Sea, you climb beyond to reach Danestream Farm Shop on your right. This has a forecourt where it just might be possible to obtain permission to park and thus cut out the preceding road walk — at any rate, there is no harm in asking!

Immediately beyond the garden centre turn right to follow what begins as a narrow metalled byway flanked by farm buildings on your right. Tarmac soon gives way to gravel and this in turn, beyond a gateway, changes to grass as your route, a public footpath, heads gently downhill. Where the main track swings right through a gate to enter a field, continue left-ahead along a fenced grass path with trees to your left, as far as another field gateway. Pass through this to follow the left-hand edge of a pasture. This brings you to a stile preceding a wooden footbridge over the Danes Stream. Beyond this your tree-shaded path rises between fences to another stile and a further fenced section along the right-hand edge of a paddock. A third stile flanked by a footpath sign brings you out on to a lane. As you follow this right-handed, it immediately bends left to head north past scattered dwellings and horse paddocks. You next cross a metalled road to follow a gravel drive signposted as a public footpath. By the entrance to Broadley Farm, on your right, this driveway ends at the New Forest's edge, where a metal step on one of the bars of a locked gate ahead of you serves as a stile.

Cross this to reach the open forest, where you walk ahead for a few yards across grass to reach and follow right-handed a narrow but clearly-defined footpath. Where visible signs of a footpath end, continue ahead across grass towards gorse bushes straight ahead, then, by a telephone post, turn right to join a Forest-edge gravel track which you follow left-handed. This fairly soon joins a metalled road, which you follow ahead for a few yards before turning left where a 40mph speed restriction sign is painted on the road surface.

A gravelly path now leads you downhill through scattered gorse clumps, dividing and reuniting once before reaching a fork where you bear right to join and follow left-handed a path from a car park on your right. Your path now angles downhill through clumps of gorse, with views across the valley ahead towards the rising sprawl of woodland called Set Thorns Inclosure.

After converging with a path from your right, you cross the Avon Water rivulet by a wooden, handrailed footbridge, just to the left of which is a gravel-bottomed ford where horse-riders cross. Set Thorns Inclosure now looms ahead. The track that leads on into it becomes gravelled as it climbs between well-spaced pines, with thicker woodland on either hand. Here, on a breezy day in autumn, we sought out a sheltered corner where a fallen tree provided us with a seat for picnic lunch before continuing uphill, where we took the second ride turning left through tallish pines and dense young conifers.

This leads to a T-junction of rides where you turn right. Where an oak-bordered clearing appears ahead fork left to join a gravel road which you follow to the left. A succession of oaks intermixed with hollies, dense young conifers, open areas, and a grove of tall hill-slope conifers rising impressively to your right flanks the woodland gravel road that now leads you towards where well-spaced oaks give shelter to a caravan camping site.

You now follow a track that bears left towards a gateway through which you leave Set Thorns Inclosure and head towards an arch underneath the old Brockenhurst-Ringwood railway. On the near side of this bear left again to follow a twisty track heading westward over gorse-and-brackeny heathland parallel with the former railway, with leftward views across the Avon Water valley towards wooded higher ground beyond. This brings you to an unfenced road which you follow to the left, keeping to parallel heathland tracks before bridging the Avon Water again.

Beyond this follow a gravel road right-handed through a gateway into Wootton Copse Inclosure. At a fork not far ahead you leave the gravel and bear left to follow a grass ride which soon joins another ride. It was while following this last ride right-ahead that we saw fallow deer as they burst out of rideside trees not far in front of us, raced up the ride for a few yards and then disappeared right-handed into thick cover once again.

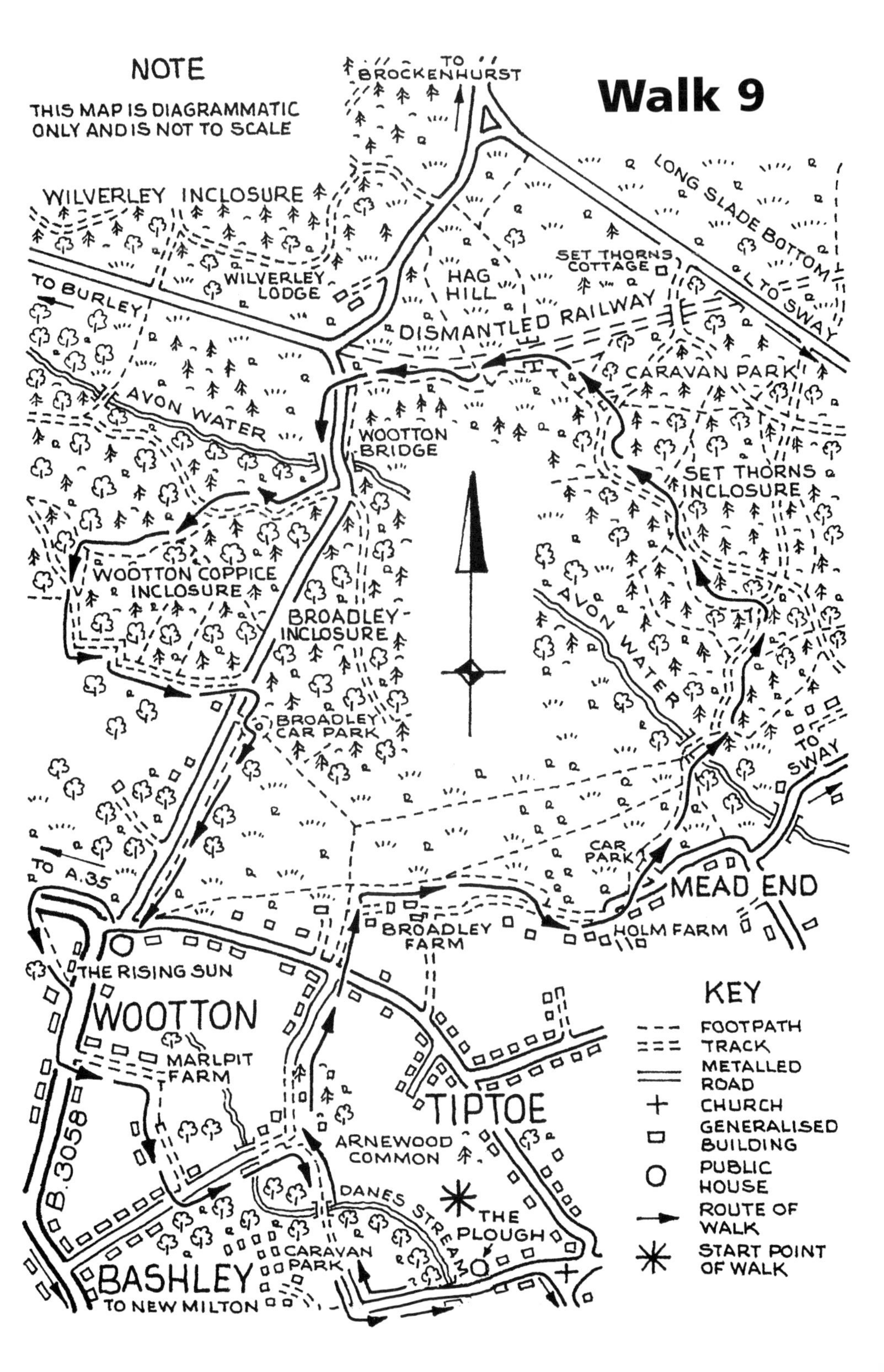

NOTE
THIS MAP IS DIAGRAMMATIC ONLY AND IS NOT TO SCALE
Walk 9
TO BROCKENHURST
WILVERLEY INCLOSURE
LONG SLADE BOTTOM
WILVERLEY LODGE
HAG HILL
SET THORNS COTTAGE
TO BURLEY
DISMANTLED RAILWAY
TO SWAY
CARAVAN PARK
AVON WATER
WOOTTON BRIDGE
SET THORNS INCLOSURE
WOOTTON COPPICE INCLOSURE
BROADLEY INCLOSURE
AVON WATER
BROADLEY CAR PARK
TO SWAY
TO A.35
CAR PARK
MEAD END
BROADLEY FARM
HOLM FARM
THE RISING SUN
WOOTTON
KEY
FOOTPATH
TRACK
METALLED ROAD
CHURCH
GENERALISED BUILDING
PUBLIC HOUSE
ROUTE OF WALK
START POINT OF WALK
MARLPIT FARM
TIPTOE
B.3058
ARNEWOOD COMMON
DANES STREAM
THE PLOUGH
CARAVAN PARK
BASHLEY
TO NEW MILTON

Set Thorns Inclosure

We last saw them close to a ride-fork where you bear left to follow an uphill ride which joins a gravel track. Follow the latter left-handed along the scenic southern margin of this inclosure in which oaks and pines provide a placid prospect to please the eye at every turn. This brings you back on to the road by which you crossed the Avon Water. From Broadley car park, on the road's far side, bear right to follow a heathland path uphill, parallel with the road, to The Rising Sun at Wootton, now directly ahead.

When you reach the pub turn right to head west in the Holmsley direction alongside the B3058. A little way along this, on your left, a public footpath sign precedes two stepless stiles which you cross to follow the right-hand edge of a paddock. At the end of this two further stepless stiles are followed by a fenced path with a ditch to your right. This leads to another stepless stile beyond which you continue across an area of rough grass with a house to the left of it to emerge over another stile on to a road, which you follow right-handed through the northern end of Bashley.

About 200 yards along this road, turn left by a postal pillar-box where a footpath sign points your way along tall-hedged Marlpits Lane. Follow this for a short distance to another footpath sign by a stile in a gap in the hedge to your right. Cross this stile and follow the right-hand edge of a muddy paddock to a further stile preceding a gravel lane. This leads ahead to a T-junction with a metalled lane, which you follow left-handed past a right-hand wood and across a tree-lined dip where you bridge the upper reaches of our old friend, the Danes Stream.

Your lane becomes briefly gravelled before bringing you to the point where it takes a right-angled turn to the left and where you turn right by a footpath sign you will recognise from the walk's outward stage. Cross the stile alongside this to follow the fenced path beyond, past a right-hand paddock to a second stile followed by a tree-lined descent to the footbridge over the Danes Stream which you previously crossed. Cross the stile beyond this to follow the right-hand side of a pasture to a gateway beyond which a fenced grass track leads you on ahead. After the track becomes gravelled, then metalled, you re-emerge past Danestream Farm Shop on to B3055, which you follow left-handed, with due care, for the final few hundred yards back to The Plough Inn at Tiptoe.

Alongside Christchurch Harbour and over Hengistbury Head

WALK 10
Allow 3 hours
5 miles
Walk begins page 61

Background to the Walk

Focusing upon one of the most scenic and popular recreational walking areas in the immediate neighbourhood of Christchurch and Bournemouth, this walk is also a journey into prehistory. Hengistbury Head, overlooking the broad spread of Christchurch Harbour in which the Dorset Stour and the Hampshire Avon unite before reaching the sea, is more than a mere promontory. As far back as the Bronze Age people recognised its value as a stronghold which could be readily defended as well as a landing place for vessels bringing merchandise from abroad. The sheltered anchorage offered by the water on the landward side and the view-commanding heights of the headland itself combined to offer unique advantages of which warring invaders and others made full use at different periods.

Hengistbury Head today is a place of peace. Footpaths wind their way over heathy heights where wayside seats invite you to pause and enjoy views without equal along this stretch of our southern shoreline. On breezy days a boisterous Channel contrasts with the calm, near-landlocked harbour in the opposite direction. In clear weather the seaward panorama extends from The Needles cliffs on the Isle of Wight, to your left, across to their Dorset mirror-image, thrusting out to Old Harry rock at The Foreland, south of Studland.

Inland, directly below you, Christchurch Harbour spreads like a lake. On its far side is Stanpit Marsh, a bird reserve of major importance, while the value of the near shoreline and its hinterland as a sanctuary for wild nature is also of a very high order. The headland

Maps
Landranger 1:50,000
Sheet 195
Pathfinder 1:25,000
or Outdoor Leisure Map
Map Reference of Start/Finish
SZ149922

How to get there
Your starting point, The Riverside pub at Tuckton, is situated alongside the River Stour halfway between Christchurch and Southbourne. From Southampton follow A3024 and then A35 around Totton and Lyndhurst, across the New Forest and along Christchurch bypass. After skirting Christchurch proper turn left at the first traffic lights to follow B3059, Stour Road, half-a-mile along which, immediately after crossing the River Stour, you will see The Riverside pub on your right. From Bournemouth follow A35 (Christchurch Road) east to Iford roundabout, where you take the third exit to follow Iford Road, leading on via Iford Lane to join Tuckton Road, which you follow left to the first roundabout. Take the first exit and within a few yards you will reach The Riverside pub on your left. Trains from Southampton to Christchurch can be used to connect with Yellow Buses on

service 22 from Somerford and Christchurch or, during the day, service 23 from Christchurch, passing The Riverside pub at Tuckton en route to Bournemouth. At Bournemouth these buses serving Tuckton start from Gervis Place, near the Central Gardens.

Pub facilities
The Riverside
This Whitbread Brewer's Fayre pub has its own riverside garden on the south bank of the Dorset Stour and a large car park where pub-using walkers may leave their cars, but please ask first. (Alternative parking space is available alongside Wick Lane, the first road that turns left after crossing the Stour from the Christchurch direction.) Opening hours are 1100-2300 on weekdays and as usual on Sundays. A restaurant licence enables food to be ordered between 1200-2200 and drinks may be served with meals. Real ales include Flower's Original and Boddington's. Murphy's Irish Stout, Guinness, and Strongbow and Woodpecker ciders are also on draught. Menu specialities include home made soup, egg mayonnaise, beef and potato pie, cauliflower cheese, seafood lasagne, brunch grills, and breaded lemon sole served with chips or new potatoes or vegetables and salad. Among other dishes featured are vegetable lasagne, mushroom and nut fetuccini, and beef and ale pie. Daily specials are listed on a board. Separate bars for smokers and non-smokers, brick alcoves with upholstered seats and tables, and leadlight windows looking

Wildfowl pond on Hengistbury Head

itself is where many summer bird visitors to this country first make landfall after crossing the English Channel and where they gather before departure in the autumn, when the possibility of obtaining a glimpse of rare species is always present.

Where the combined waters of the Stour and the Avon reach the sea between Hengistbury Head and Mudeford is the tide-race called The Run. There licensed fishermen spread their nets in due season to harvest some of the salmon which enter the harbour on their way upriver to spawn. Inland, just beyond where the rivers which feed the harbour merge, Christchurch Priory Church stands proud above a scene it has dominated for the past 800 years. Near by is the Norman castle of the town anciently called Twynham from its situation between two rivers and, little less prominent, waterfront buildings which owe nothing to antiquity and everything to what has been deemed architecturally appropriate to one of the oldest towns in Wessex by 20th century planners and builders.

Bournemouth, to the west, was largely created by the railway. Even so, the very first railway steered a wide berth around the area, reaching Dorchester via Ringwood, with a single line branch to Christchurch which was later extended to Bournemouth. Direct rail access from London arrived in 1888 with the completion of the line between Brockenhurst and Christchurch by way of New Milton. By then, the heathy, sandy wilderness which separated Christchurch and Poole right up to the middle of the 19th century had been extensively built over. There has been much further building since.

out on to the river are other features. A children's play area includes Charlie Chalk's Fun Factory and other well-tried favourites of the younger generation.

Walk 10

Distance: ***Allow 3 hours for this 5-mile walk.***

From The Riverside pub at Tuckton cross adjacent Stour Road to follow a macadamised path through a boatyard opposite. This leads to the south bank of the Stour, an inlet of which you skirt to follow a gravel path through tree-dotted pleasure grounds adjoining the boat-crowded river. Where a path continues ahead cross a wooden footbridge on your left and carry on along the river bank to where the gravel path ends.

Now continue across the grass ahead to where River House and its private grounds confront you at a point where you bear right, away from the river, to a resumed gravel path which follows a fenced course between two swing-gates. Gravel gives way to grass as you then follow the leftward edge of a pasture to the next swing-gate, beyond which a raised gravel path crosses a field to a further swing-gate preceding a wooden footbridge over a reedy water channel. Christchurch Priory looms beyond the river to your left as you now pass through yet another swing-gate to enter Wick Fields and Reed Beds, a nationally important feeding and resting area for migrating birds, as a notice points out.

Here your path, no longer gravelled, bears diagonally right to cross an area of rough pasture dotted with brambles, bushes and gorse clumps. After passing through the next swing-gate you repeat the process, angling right, away from the left-hand fence, beyond which are the reed-margined upper reaches of Christchurch Harbour. You now head for another swing-gate where you emerge on to a tarmac drive leading to Hengistbury Outdoor Education and Field Study Centre, the green-roofed building on your left.

Cross the metalled driveway just to the right of the entrance gate to the field study centre to follow a path through a gorsey area and emerge on to another metalled road, which you follow ahead. The compound surrounding the thatched buildings to your right here serves as a stable for the road-train which offers the sole means of wheeled access to the beach chalets opposite Mudeford, at the eastern end of the headland. This shuttles to and fro throughout the day in the holiday season and at other times.

Alongside the road you now follow is a seat facing the harbour: an ideal place to pause for a preliminary spy to see what birds may be in evidence. Crows and mallard, Britain's most common wild duck, were species most conspicuous on the day when we did this walk, but there is always an excellent chance of something extra special.

The River Stour at Tuckton, dominated by the Priory

Follow the road to where it bends right into a wood. At this point you branch off to follow a gravel path left-ahead through scrub oaks and over rough pasture with the harbour to your left. Where a discernible footpath ends follow the harbour's shingly shore to where a path presently resumes. A wooden footbridge takes you across a creek which snakes in from the harbour. Oystercatchers along the tideline took little notice of our passing as we continued to where the path rejoins the metalled road at the turnaround point for the road-train by the beach chalets which line the sandy shore here.

Follow the road right-handed to where it soon bends right, then go left-ahead along a footway beside the chalets to climb a stepped path to the higher ground of Hengistbury Head. At the top is a seat from which you can look back across the harbour-mouth to Mudeford, beyond which Highcliffe Castle peeps out above the clifftop. A guest there in Edwardian times was Germany's Kaiser Wilhelm II. During his stay he attended Sunday service at Christchurch Priory, in which a notice preserved to this day advised the regular congregation how to comport themselves in the awe-inspiring presence of H. I. M.

Where the high ground path soon triplicates follow the left-hand gravel path. A fence to the left of this marks the limit of safe movement in that direction, where cliff erosion has been attacking the once solid soil of the upper headland. A small lake lies in a dip to your right as you carry on up to a crossing of tracks where you turn left to pass a lookout station of H.M. Coastguard. A seat just beyond this, on your right, gives a grandstand view across the harbour where, on a summer's day, pleasure craft ceaselessly make their way to and from the open Channel. In the holiday season, too, a ferry operates between Christchurch and the harbour mouth opposite Mudeford, across which another ferry gives access to and from the Hengistbury side of The Run.

The path becomes metalled, then stepped, descending steeply as you follow it to a fork where you bear left to follow a wide coast path to the south end of Double Dykes, a 2,000-year-old Celtic earthwork protecting the western approach to the headland. A notice reminds us how laboriously this must have been constructed by an army of men using hand tools and baskets to dig and carry the soil, with

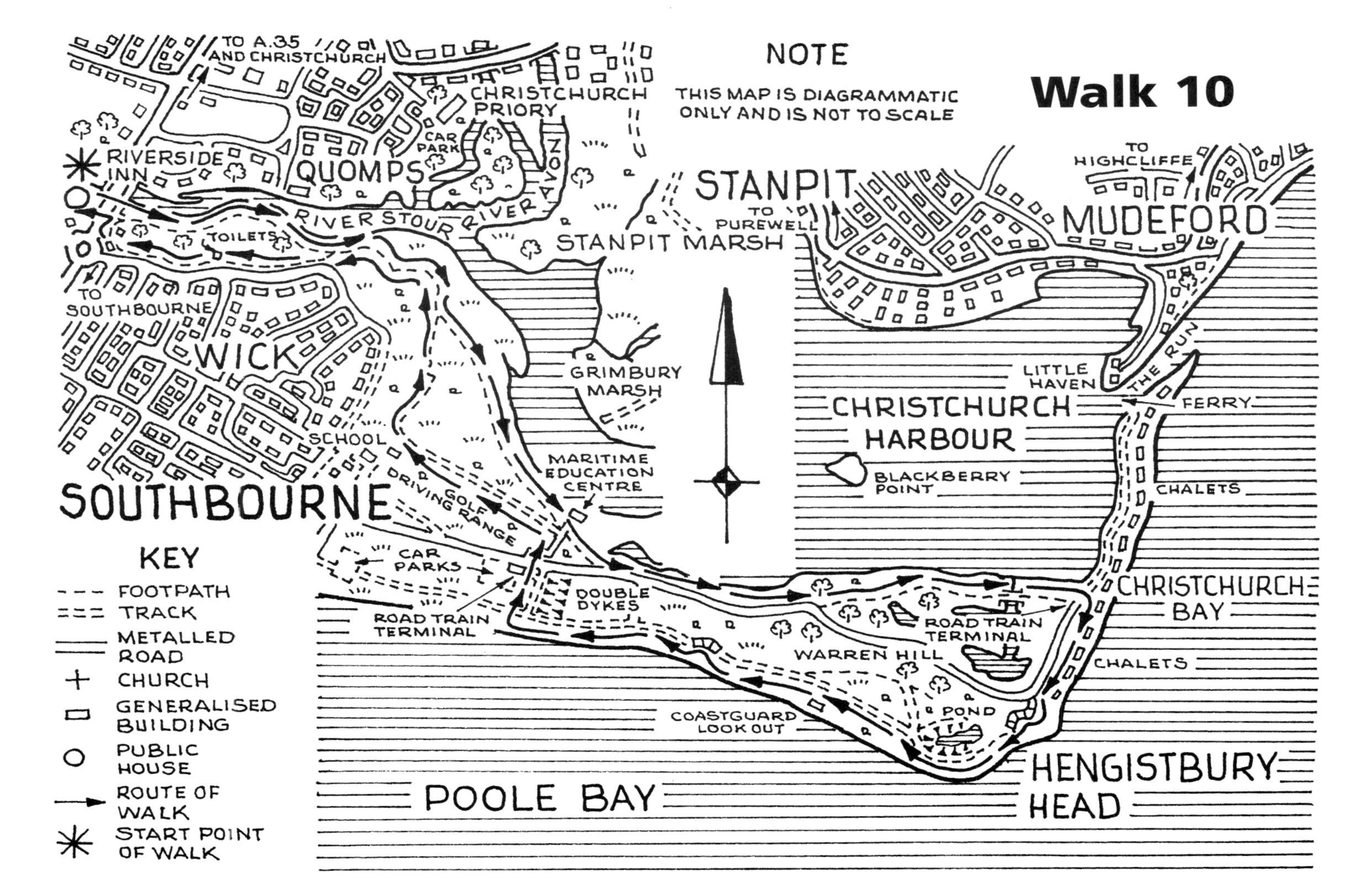
Walk 10
NOTE
THIS MAP IS DIAGRAMMATIC ONLY AND IS NOT TO SCALE
TO A.35 AND CHRISTCHURCH
CHRISTCHURCH PRIORY
CAR PARK
RIVERSIDE INN
QUOMPS
RIVER AVON
RIVER STOUR
TOILETS
STANPIT
TO PUREWELL
STANPIT MARSH
TO HIGHCLIFFE
MUDEFORD
TO SOUTHBOURNE
WICK
GRIMBURY MARSH
LITTLE HAVEN
THE RUN
FERRY
CHRISTCHURCH HARBOUR
SCHOOL
MARITIME EDUCATION CENTRE
BLACKBERRY POINT
CHALETS
SOUTHBOURNE
GOLF DRIVING RANGE
CAR PARKS
DOUBLE DYKES
CHRISTCHURCH BAY
ROAD TRAIN TERMINAL
ROAD TRAIN TERMINAL
WARREN HILL
CHALETS
POND
COASTGUARD LOOK OUT
HENGISTBURY HEAD
POOLE BAY
KEY
FOOTPATH
TRACK
METALLED ROAD
CHURCH
GENERALISED BUILDING
PUBLIC HOUSE
ROUTE OF WALK
START POINT OF WALK

Christchurch Harbour from Hengistbury Head

some assistance from ox-wagons for the heavier haulage involved.

Turn right to follow a path alongside this earthwork to the metalled road used by the road-train. Cross this to join and follow a narrow road to the near side of the gateway to Hengistbury Field Study Centre. Here you turn left around the first of two gates on that side to follow a semi-derelict metalled track, with a golf course to your left and a wooden fence to your right. When you reach a scissors-crossing of tracks continue towards a building left-ahead (Solent Coffee Shop, 'open all day'), from which you turn right to a swing-gate. Pass through this to follow a path along the leftward edge of rough pasture — Wick Fields again — with a fence on your left-hand side.

Go left through the next swing-gate to cross a marshy, sluggish stream by a concrete bridge and then immediately cross a stile on your right and a plank bridge over the ditch beyond. You now bear left to follow a narrow path between bushes on your right and the ditch to your left, emerging from which your path angles right in line with Christchurch Priory, ahead, to join and follow left-handed the raised gravel path you followed on the outward stage of the walk. Gravel ceases as you enter the next field, the right-hand edge of which you follow to where a gravelled way resumes and curves left as a fenced path between swing-gates.

Emerging just left of River House and to the right of Wick Farm and its buildings, cross the riverside recreation ground to follow the river-bank path left-handed. Where this path fairly soon divides keep left to follow a metalled footpath along the left-hand edge of the timbered pleasure ground. After skirting left of a public convenience and of an ice-cream sales booth you will emerge past the boatyard first encountered on to Stour Road, which you cross to retrieve your car from The Riverside pub car park.

Paths and Green Lanes near Sopley

WALK 11
At least 3 hours
5 miles
Walk begins page 67

Background to the Walk

Until late Saxon times the countryside extending all the way from The Weald, in Kent, Surrey and Sussex, across Hampshire and well into Dorset was almost continuous forest. The New Forest, as we now know it, had yet to be named. The larger wasteland of which it formed part was called Ytene, supposedly meaning 'the country of the Jutes', which suggests that Jutes, rather than Saxons, originally wrested much of it from its native British inhabitants and established their settlements in it.

These would have necessitated clearings in the forest which were identified in placenames by the common suffix 'ley' (Old English 'leah'). Recorded in Domesday Book as 'Sopelie', the village name Sopley probably originated to define a forest clearing owned by a man called Soppa. On the other hand, 'soppa' was apparently an Old English word meaning 'marsh', so perhaps the clearing was merely a moist one. This would hardly be surprising, for the countryside hereabouts is very flat and the River Avon, famously flood-prone — in winter especially — flows close by.

This early, forest-fringed settlement undoubtedly had a church: a wooden structure in the first instance, and almost certainly located on the slight eminence where stands the Church of St Michael and All Angels, serving the parish of Sopley today. Begun in the 13th century, the squat-towered, stone-walled building contains several sculptures of that period or perhaps of the 14th century. The usual memorials to leading local families are in evidence. One such family, named Willis, owned adjacent Sopley Park and supplied two

Maps
Landranger 1:50,000
Sheet 195
Pathfinder 1:25,000
or Outdoor Leisure Map
Map Reference of Start/Finish
SZ157969

How to get there
Sopley lies just over 3 miles north of Christchurch on B3347, the old, direct main road between Ringwood and Christchurch. From Southampton head west along A3024 and then along A35 around Lyndhurst, via Holmsley and along Christchurch bypass, which you follow as far as a roundabout where you take the third exit to head north along B3347 past Burton and via Winkton to Sopley, the next village, where The Woolpack lies on your right. From Bournemouth follow Wessex Way to Cooper Dean roundabout where you filter left to take the third exit, A3060. At the next roundabout bear left to follow A35 around Christchurch and for a short distance along Christchurch bypass before turning left to follow B3347 north, as directed above. Buses on Solent Blue Line/Wilts & Dorset services X1 and X2 from Southampton via

Lyndhurst and Cadnam respectively connect at Ringwood with Wilts & Dorset services 105 and 115 passing through Sopley en route to Christchurch and Bournemouth. By the same token, these latter bus services give direct access to Sopley from Bournemouth and Christchurch and, in the case of service 105, also from Poole.

Pub facilities
The Woolpack.
Open all day on weekdays from 1100-2300 and at the usual hours on Sundays, this very popular pub, which dates from the 17th century and was once a coaching inn, takes food orders between 1200-1400 and between 1830 (1900 on Sundays)-2130. Real ales include Ringwood Bitter, Wadworth 6X and Marston Pedigree Bitter. Also on draught are Whitbread Best Bitter, Guinness, Murphy's Irish Stout and Stonehouse cider. The lunch menu will tempt you with dishes such as salmon in white wine, turkey breast with port and apricot sauce, haddock and prawn Florentine, lamb noisettes in a dijonnaise sauce, half a roast chicken with apricot stuffing, cod and broccoli au gratin, rainbow trout and prawns in lemon butter sauce, braised steak in red wine, onions and cream, all served with vegetables and potatoes, or a choice of 4 salads. Daily specials might feature, say, whole fresh Mudeford lobster or fresh mussels in white wine, garlic and cream with granary bread. There is also a good choice of desserts. Children are admitted except in the bar area. You will find

The Woolpack at Sopley

vicars to add to a list of known incumbents dating back to 1308.

More recent items of special interest include a model Vietnamese fishing-boat. This was made and given as a token of gratitude for local hospitality by refugee boat people from that corner of south-east Asia, 600 of whom were accommodated for a time in the old RAF camp on the Bransgore side of Sopley after arriving in England in 1979. Another handsome church embellishment is a 1984 tapestry with Sopley as its subject.

Sopley Mill, just behind the church, has a history stretching back over many centuries. Water from the mill stream still flushes vigorously through it but has long since ceased to turn a mill-wheel. It provides a pleasing visual adjunct to premises which now function as a fashionable restaurant.

Sopley's old world cottages include a number of thatched ones and crowd close to a narrow main road which now forms part of a one-way traffic system through the village. The Woolpack itself is thatched and lies in the 'island' created by the modern through traffic arrangements. A second village pub was closed down years ago and is now a private dwelling, but Sopley is still the lucky possessor of a village stores and post office.

The original forest character of the countryside hereabouts is attested by another placename, that of the small village or hamlet of Ripley, lying somewhat off

no fruit machines or jukebox, but on Thursday lunchtimes and Saturday evenings Sylvia King performs on the piano and on Sunday evenings in winter a local 'amdrams' group entertains with 'songs from the stars'. Two open fires enhance winter comfort. The pub garden overlooks a substantial brook with a complement of ducks. The large car park fills up quickly at weekends, and walkers using the pub should ask first before leaving their cars there.

Sopley Church

the beaten track along lanes east of the Avon Valley and which you skirt in the course of this walk. The clearing there, experts tell us, would have been strip-shaped, as also will have applied in the case of at least two other Ripleys: one in Surrey and another in Derbyshire. You will also pass within sight of the outskirts of Bransgore, a forest-edge village of no great charm but with an expanding population. Did this perhaps first come into being as a triangular plot of land, or 'gore', owned by someone called Bran or similar?

Walk 11

Distance: ***Allow at least 3 hours for this five mile walk.***
From The Woolpack head south for a few yards to the junction where the one way traffic system reunites towards the Christchurch end of Sopley and there turn right to follow a short cul-de-sac for a look at the ruggedly stone-built Church of St Michael and All Angels. If there are problems about parking your car at the pub while doing the walk there is alternative space near here and elsewhere in Sopley. Just behind and below the church is Sopley Mill, now revamped as a restaurant specialising in four-course dinners. The water rushing beneath it is a sidestream of the Avon, whose many-channelled course spreads across a half-mile width and more of the flat land west of Sopley.

After this short initial digression walk back to the main road and follow it left, past The Woolpack once more and so northward past the village stores and post office, on your left. If you want to learn more about local lore than I have sketched out by way of introducing the setting for this walk, a local author has published a village history which is on sale here.

Not many yards farther on a sign points out where The Avon Valley Path turns off right-handed. This relatively new long-distance walk linking Christchurch and Salisbury passes through Sopley village centre before resuming a footpath

Quiet countryside near Sopley

course here, where you cross a stile and head north with a hedgerow to your left and a picturesque tree-bordered brook to your right. This brook is the selfsame one which flows through the garden of The Woolpack. It has its source in the New Forest, among the moors and oozy bogs which sprawl on the Ringwood side of Burley, and by the time it reaches Sopley it has grown to a mini-river which then spills into the Avon.

A second stile precedes a field, the right-hand edge of which you follow to a third stile, which you cross to follow a fenced path to a fourth stile. This served as a seat near the grass-bordered brook for picnic lunch enjoyed in sunshine after a shower on the autumn day when we tried this walk. While keeping a weather eye well open for more rainclouds — none materialised — we were glad of the comforting proximity of the oaks.

Not many yards farther on a wicket-gate leads out on to a narrow country lane. The Avon Valley Path follows this leftward, but you cross it to follow another signposted brookside path through trees. This leads ahead to a stile around which you walk to follow the right-hand edge of an arable field. You then head through more trees to emerge on to another lane, which you cross to follow a path over a stile and along the right-hand margin of another arable field. Towards the far end of this your path heads into streamside oaks to your right to join another path at right-angles to your own.

Follow this right-handed over a stream bridge, a short distance beyond which your new path becomes a lane. This leads past houses to a T-junction of lanes at the northern end of Ripley. Here you angle left to cross the lane ahead and pass through a wicket-gate to follow a hedged green lane. Signposted as a footpath, this follows a fairly straight course in an easterly direction. Mature trees to your left contrast with newly planted ones to your right for a few hundred yards until taller wayside timber flanks your route on that side also.

A plank bridge over a small stream is followed soon by a gate with a notice:

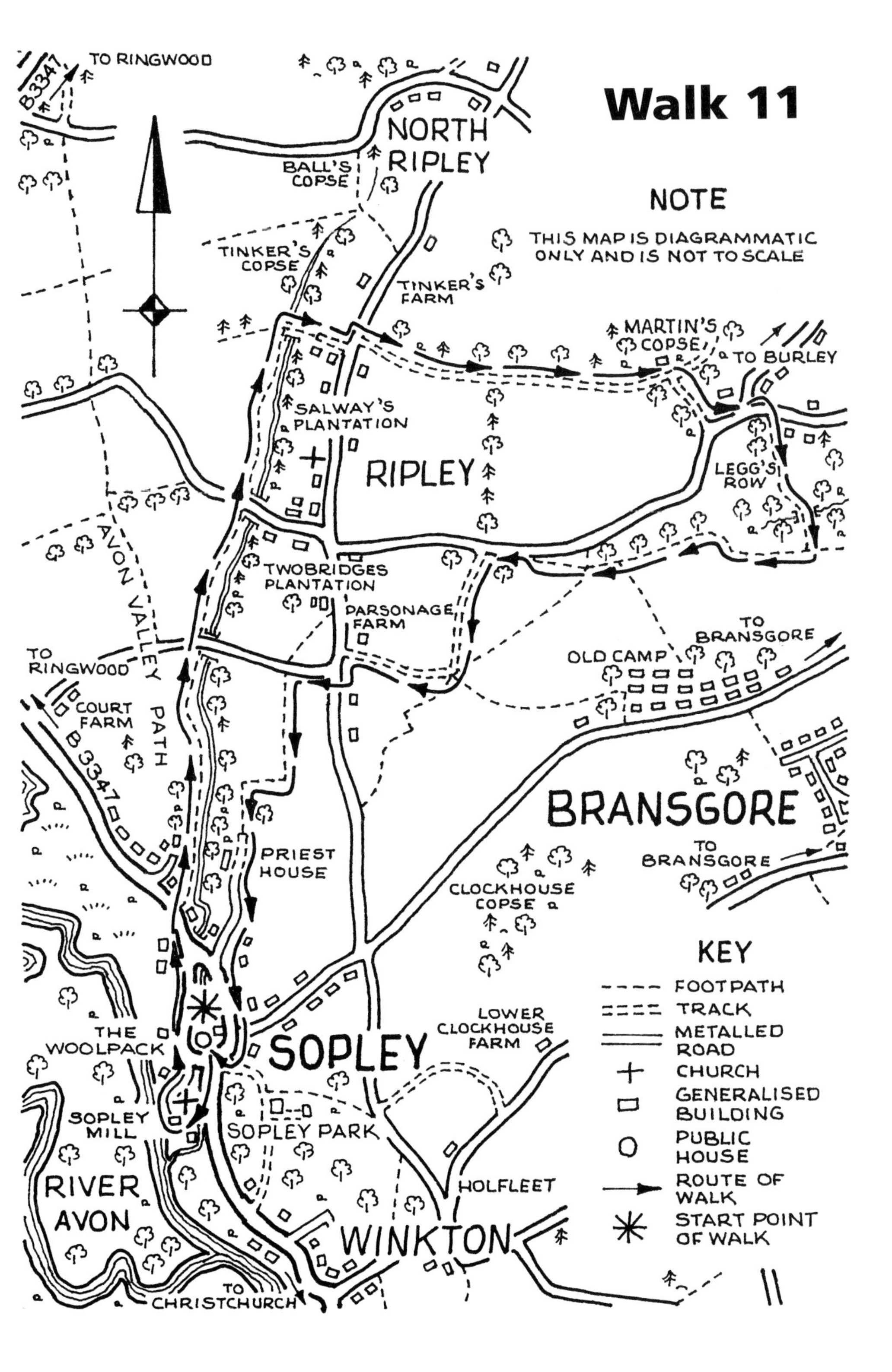
Walk 11
NOTE
THIS MAP IS DIAGRAMMATIC ONLY AND IS NOT TO SCALE
TO RINGWOOD
B3347
NORTH RIPLEY
BALL'S COPSE
TINKER'S COPSE
TINKER'S FARM
MARTIN'S COPSE
TO BURLEY
SALWAY'S PLANTATION
RIPLEY
LEGG'S ROW
TWOBRIDGES PLANTATION
PARSONAGE FARM
AVON VALLEY PATH
TO RINGWOOD
COURT FARM
B 3347
OLD CAMP
TO BRANSGORE
BRANSGORE
PRIEST HOUSE
CLOCKHOUSE COPSE
TO BRANSGORE
KEY
FOOTPATH
TRACK
METALLED ROAD
CHURCH
GENERALISED BUILDING
PUBLIC HOUSE
ROUTE OF WALK
START POINT OF WALK
THE WOOLPACK
SOPLEY
LOWER CLOCKHOUSE FARM
SOPLEY MILL
SOPLEY PARK
HOLFLEET
RIVER AVON
WINKTON
TO CHRISTCHURCH

Sopley village

'horse riding prohibited'. Beyond this you pass a galvanised iron building set back into woodland on your left and join a gravel lane which you follow right-handed to another gate preceding a metalled lane.

Follow the lane left-handed for a few yards to where it forks, and here bear right. Within a few more yards a signposted, well-used footpath leads you right-handed through trees to a stile. After crossing this you follow the right-hand edge of a pasture, bearing left with it at the far end to reach and cross a stream footbridge and a stile on your right-hand side. Follow the right-hand edge of the next pasture to a stile by another footpath sign, on your right. Crossing this, with houses on the edge of Bransgore visible just beyond trees to your left, you now follow a well-defined path along the right-hand edge of a meadow, with an oak-bordered stream directly to your right.

Three further stiles with intervening pastures precede a woody footpath section. Along this a low stile precedes in its turn a handrailed footbridge over a brook and a further stile, beyond which a clear path follows the right-hand edge of an arable field. A gap through a hedge leads into a further arable field, midway along the right-hand edge of which you cross a stile on your right to emerge on to a narrow metalled lane. Follow this left-handed for perhaps 150 yards before turning left to follow a hedged green lane signposted as a byway.

Where this latter joins a field-access track emerging from your left, the two combined swing right. The hedged track you now follow becomes metalled just before joining a metalled lane, which you follow left-handed for a few yards before turning right to follow another hedged lane. Carry on along this metalled byway as far as a slight bend to the right where you cross a stile on your left. A wide unploughed headland forms your path along the left-hand side of an arable field, with a high-fenced grass field to your left. At the field's far end your path bends right with it to the far corner from where you first entered the field, where you cross a stile on your left.

You now follow a hedged path with overhanging trees which soon becomes a green lane. This in turn becomes metalled as you pass 17th century Priest House, a bed-and-breakfast establishment on your right, beyond which you carry on ahead to reach the main road once more in Sopley. Turn left here and then circle right to find your way back to The Woolpack and its car park, or to the cul-de-sac which leads to the church, if that is where you left your car.

Footpaths and Forest near Ringwood

WALK 12
Allow 3 hours
5 1/4 miles
Walk begins page 73

Maps
Landranger 1:50,000
Sheet 195
Pathfinder 1:25,000
or Outdoor Leisure Map
Map Reference of Start/Finish
SU163048

How to get there
The Elm Tree Inn lies at the junction of Hightown Road and Crow Lane, on the south-eastern edge of Ringwood. If heading west along A31, having reached this via A3024, M271 and M27 from the Southampton direction, take the first turning left after passing the turn-off for Burley at Picket Post and you will reach the starting-point pub after about a mile-and-a-half, on your right. If approaching from the west or from Bournemouth via Wessex Way and A338, take the Ringwood town centre exit from the roundabout where the Salisbury road joins A31 and follow B3347 for just over half-a-mile towards the southern end of Ringwood before turning left just short of the site of Ringwood's old railway station to follow Hightown Road. When you soon reach a T-junction with Eastfield Lane, turn right to carry on along Hightown Road for a very short distance until The Elm Tree appears on

Background to the Walk

The Avon Valley town of Ringwood was a royal manor in Saxon times, when it already had a church as well as a mill. In AD955 it was recorded as 'Rimucwuda', which probably meant 'a wood on a boundary'. Just which boundary this was one can only guess: certainly not that of the New Forest, as at present, because until William I 'created' it in or about the year 1079 the Forest did not exist as such but was part of a much larger semi-wilderness called 'Ytene'.

Few Saxon places of worship long survived the zeal for building new churches which swept the country in Norman times and later. Ringwood gained a new church of its own in the 13th century. Much added to and altered by later 'restorers', this was demolished and replaced by another new structure, the present one, in the 19th century. A secular Ringwood building of some interest is a pub just off the A31, The Original White Hart. This refers to a white hart, or stag, called Albert, which is supposed to have been set free in the New Forest to provide a quarry for hunting one day when Henry VII was present. The hunt went ahead as planned. Albert performed so well that when at last he would run no farther he was caught up in the watermeadows beside the Avon, just outside Ringwood, and adorned with a gold crown around his neck, thereafter to lead a charmed existence. Ringwood's White Hart pub and others up and down the country use a white stag likewise embellished as the centrepiece of their sign.

Perhaps Henry VII recalled an incident involving another white hart, this time in Blackmoor Forest, *your left. Limited stop buses on Solent Blue Line/Wilts & Dorset service X1 from Bournemouth and from Southampton via Lyndhurst and Burley and service X2, also from Bournemouth, and from Southampton via Cadnam, and on Wilts & Dorset service X3 between Bournemouth and Salisbury, pass through Ringwood, from which local buses on Wilts & Dorset services 136 and 137 to and from Poulner pass The Elm Tree.*

Pub facilities
The Elm Tree Inn
Open all day from 1100-2300 on weekdays and at the usual hours on Sundays, this picturesque thatched pub with its inglenook fireplace, beams and exposed brickwork is a grade two listed building. Originally a dairy farm, it became a pub in the 1970s. The elm tree after which it was named has vanished, like so many others. A greatly extended bar area includes what used to be the pub restaurant, there now being a bar menu only. This is changed regularly, with daily specials including dishes like lentil crumble served with a mixed salad, corned beef and potato pie with salad or roll and pickles, pancake rolls and chips, lamb and vegetable stew, and a tempting range of basket meals. Jacket potatoes, fish and chips, lasagne and chips, gammon steak, steak and ale pie, mushroom and nut fetuccini, curry and rice, game pie and various desserts are popular menu items. Children's meals are available and food orders are taken between 1200-1430 and 1900-

The Elm Tree Inn at Hightown

north Dorset, where Henry III was hunting when a stag of this colour appeared in front of hounds. When this stag was killed by others a short time afterwards the King ordered fines and imprisonment of those responsible and imposed a special land tax which continued for generations. The village of Kingstag in Blackmoor Vale marks the scene of this sad occurrence.

You just might see deer in the New Forest corner explored on this walk, but the odds are against it due to the area's popularity with walkers, who cause inevitable disturbance. You are even less likely to see a white deer, though if you do it will be a fallow deer buck, not a hart: a term confined to prime males of the red deer species, be they red in colour or otherwise.

This walk affords plenty of variety: Forest-edge farmland, hilly heathland, timbered tranquillity, sleepy suburbia — and a lake beloved of geese whose forebears came to this country from Canada and are now very much at home here. A name shared with a species of bird much in evidence in these parts is that of the Forest-fringe hamlet called Crow, where you glimpse the remnants of a railway along which express trains once ran between London, Southampton and Dorchester but which was axed by Dr Beeching in his purge of the 1960s.

Walk 12

2200. Real ales drawn from hand pumps include Wadworth 6X, Gale's HSB, Flower's Original and a guest ale. Also on draught are Heineken lager, Murphy's stout, Whitbread Best Bitter and Strongbow Dry Cider as well as chilled dry French white wine and Liebfraumilch. An adjacent former barn has been adapted as a functions room with a self-contained bar for wedding receptions and similar events. It is also used for a skittle alley and as a venue for live music. Walkers using the pub may use the pub car park.

Distance: *Allow at least 3 hours for this five-and-a-quarter mile walk.*

Leaving The Elm Tree behind you on your left, immediately cross a stile on your left, next to the pub, to follow where a footpath sign points, diagonally right-handed across a pasture, its route being waymarked through gaps in mid-field fencing. This brings you to a footbridge over a stream with a stile on its far side, which you cross and then head diagonally left to reach and cross a stile halfway along a right-hand hedge. You now follow the right-hand hedge of an oblong meadow to reach a stile leading out on to a lane bordering a residential area called Hightown.

Cross the lane and head diagonally left to follow a hedged gravel track, which heads diagonally right from the metalled byway. Signposted as a bridleway, the gravel track meanders steadily uphill between scattered dwellings very much of the 'des res' category one would expect of a Forest-edge suburb of an old country town like Ringwood. After about three-quarters of a mile you reach and cross a road to walk through a gate alongside a cattlegrid and enter the Forest itself.

You now head diagonally right from the road just crossed to follow another gravel track. This leads through scattered oaks and bracken with more 'des res' dwellings on your right, soon reaching a crossing of tracks where you continue left-ahead, with a fence at first to your right and then brackeny open forest on both sides. Next you join and follow right-ahead a semi-metalled road serving Forest-edge houses. Gravel soon re-asserts itself, and at the approach to a house where your gravel track divides, fork left.

Just past a left-hand tennis court and a house called Foulford Lodge turn right to follow a path whose commencement is flanked by two low posts. This brings you within a matter of yards to the crossing-point of five paths. Turn right here to follow a path which heads south-east across a moorland mixture of heather, fern and gorse. Having climbed from the Avon Valley, you can now look across it from high, open ground to where the hazy Purbeck Hills loom on the distant Dorset skyline, well on the other side of Bournemouth.

Your gravelly path winds down into Foulford Bottom to cross a stream there by a footbridge. Forest streams tend to be dark and well-supplied with aquatic wildlife, and this one is no exception. Pond-skaters were light-footedly walking the water when we passed.

Your path now climbs a shoulder of moorland to reach a crossing of tracks quite close to a forest car park on your left. Turn right here to join a wider, grassy track which you follow right-handed, heading south-southwest along a gorse-grown

Heathery heights near Picket Post

ridge crest. The route you are now following was probably one of several in these parts once used by smugglers. In the heart of Ridley Wood, near by, is an ancient hollow lane which is supposed to have been a meeting point for traffickers in contraband brandy, landed under cover of darkness after being shipped across from France.

Castle Hill, a moorland vantage point west of Burley, looms to your left as your track descends to join a road by scattered pine trees. Almost immediately turn right to follow a fairly well-defined path with a Forest-edge fence to your left. Within a quarter-of-a-mile this joins a track which you follow left-handed to a gate adjoined by a stile. Cross the stile to follow a fenced path to a metal gate, through which you pass to follow another fenced section of footpath. This brings you to a stile where a footpath sign points the way ahead, half-left across a lawned expanse, downhill to join a gravel driveway, which you follow ahead past a timber-fronted house called St Andrew's Lodge.

Hurn Farm and other sizeable houses in secluded grounds flank the tree-bordered driveway that now leads you north-westward, crossing en route the stream you last encountered in Foulford Bottom. Sometimes macadamised, sometimes not, the drive heads uphill to a bend, with a wood beyond, where you turn left with it. A subsequent bend to the right precedes a right-angled left-hand turn, a few yards beyond which you turn left and leave this drive to follow another along which a public footpath sign points.

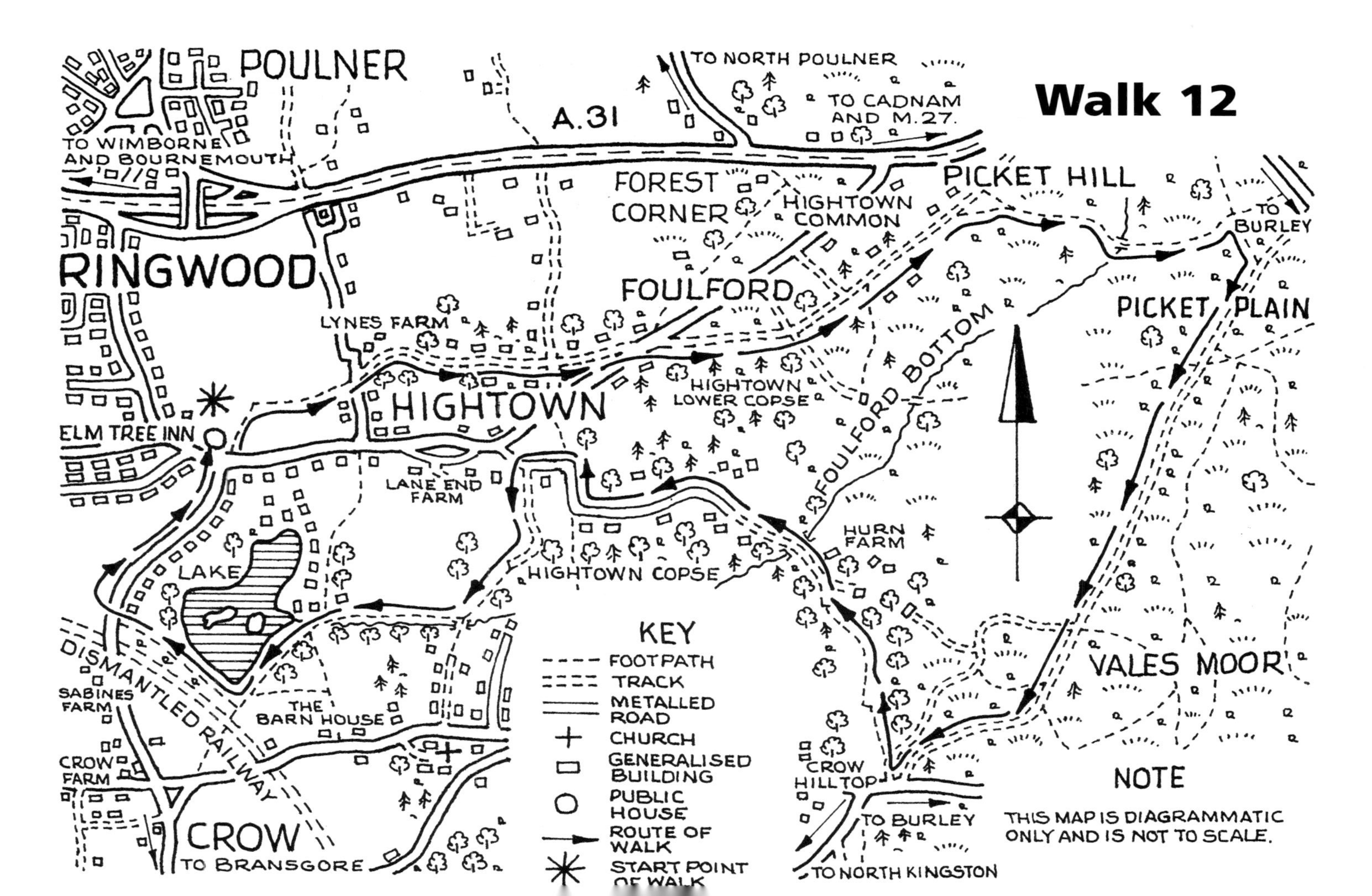
Walk 12
POULNER
TO WIMBORNE AND BOURNEMOUTH
A.31
TO NORTH POULNER
TO CADNAM AND M.27.
RINGWOOD
FOREST CORNER
HIGHTOWN COMMON
PICKET HILL
TO BURLEY
FOULFORD
LYNES FARM
PICKET PLAIN
HIGHTOWN
HIGHTOWN LOWER COPSE
ELM TREE INN
FOULFORD BOTTOM
LANE END FARM
HURN FARM
HIGHTOWN COPSE
LAKE
KEY
FOOTPATH
TRACK
METALLED ROAD
CHURCH
GENERALISED BUILDING
PUBLIC HOUSE
ROUTE OF WALK
START POINT OF WALK
VALES MOOR
DISMANTLED RAILWAY
SABINES FARM
THE BARN HOUSE
CROW FARM
CROW
TO BRANSGORE
CROW HILLTOP
TO BURLEY
TO NORTH KINGSTON
NOTE
THIS MAP IS DIAGRAMMATIC ONLY AND IS NOT TO SCALE.

Tree-fringed lake en route near Crow

Where this latter gravel drive soon ends cross a stile followed by two kissing-gates through a wooden-railed horse paddock, across which you head diagonally left-handed. Here you come close to the Foulford brook once again after crossing another stile to follow a fenced path with a tree-bordered gully on your left. From this you emerge past a building to skirt left-handed of a new housing development. You walk around the next stile to carry on along the path ahead, with the tree-shaded Foulford stream in its gully still to your left.

The stream bypasses a sizeable lake on the site of former gravel workings, with wooded islands in its middle and, when we passed, a large population of constantly honking Canada geese. We saw an even larger flock of these geese enjoying a meal of lush meadow grass in one of the pastures to our left as we followed the east bank of the lake, at the end of which your path angles sharply right to cross a rickety stile. You now enter a sheep pasture, halfway across which you pass through a metal gate before reaching a further stile. Cross this to follow the path through what we found as a brambly area flanked by gardens to the right, leading to another broken-down stile which you can walk around to join and follow metalled Crow Lane right-handed.

To avoid the stiles, sheep pasture and brambles, instead of turning right to follow the path from the lake's southern end you can join the parallel course of what you may hardly now recognise as the old Southampton-Dorchester railway. The derelict stretch of it in question once ran from Brockenhurst via Ringwood and Wimborne to merge with the present Bournemouth route at Hamworthy Junction, west of Poole. Known as Castleman's Corkscrew after the Wimborne solicitor who contrived its tortuous route to bypass the heart of the New Forest while also serving his home town, this was closed in the 1960s as part of the railway rationalisation instigated by Dr Beeching when he was chairman of British Rail.

Having emerged directly opposite where Crow Arch Lane diverges west, turn right and follow Crow Lane north for a quarter-of-a-mile to where The Elm Tree looms ahead, facing Crow Lane's junction with Hightown Road.

Avon Valley Paths Around Ibsley

WALK 13
At least 4 hours
7 miles
Walk begins page 78

Background to the Walk

Ibsley is one of those places where the term 'old' has special meaning. The little Avon Valley village already existed when William the Conqueror was rubbing in the fact of his conquest by having a detailed inventory taken of what he had gained through winning the Battle of Hastings. In his Domesday survey it featured as 'Tibeslei', meaning 'woodland clearing of a man called Tibbi or Ibbi', a personal name known from other evidence to have been in use at that time. Two hundred years later it was recorded afresh as 'Ibeslehe'.

Most of Ibsley's dwellings today are strikingly redolent of antiquity. Times past are reflected in house names: The Old Rectory, The Old Bailiff's House, The Old Smithy, The Old Post Office — each a reminder of departed village vitality as a self-dependent working community. Ibsley today, like many another small country village, slumbers as peacefully as the traffic streaming through it will permit, with the pub, and little else, as a surviving hub of activity. Even the little church, built in 1832, is now closed.

The three-arched bridge across the Avon here is robust and enduring, which is just as well in view of its being the only public means of crossing the river on wheels between Ringwood and Fordingbridge.

Beyond the Avon looms Harbridge church, which was built in 1838 though the tower is older and conspicuous not just as the dominating feature in an otherwise level landscape but because of the stair-turret which surmounts it. The prefix 'Har' in 'Harbridge' perhaps derives from the Old English 'heord' meaning herds or flocks and, hence, a crossing-

Maps
Landranger 1:50,000
Sheet 195
Pathfinder 1:25,000
Sheets SU 00/10 & SU 01/11
or Outdoor Leisure Map
Map Reference of Start/Finish
SU150093

How to get there
Ibsley is on A338 halfway between Fordingbridge and Ringwood. From Southampton follow A3024, M271 and westbound M27 to Cadnam, B3079 to Brook, B3078 from there to Fordingbridge and southbound A338 from there to Ibsley, or follow A3024, M271, westbound M27 and A31 to Ringwood and northbound A338 from there to Ibsley. Leave Bournemouth via Wessex Way to follow A338 to Ringwood, briefly joining A31 there before resuming A338 to Ibsley. Solent Blue Line/Wilts & Dorset buses on services X1 and X2 between Southampton, Bournemouth and Poole connect at Ringwood with Wilts & Dorset service X3 between Poole, Bournemouth and Salisbury, calling at Ibsley.

place for farm livestock over the otherwise sparsely-bridged river. Bickton, a little way upstream, probably started as a placename to mark a farm holding by someone called Bica. North and South Gorley, east of the river, are typical small Forest-fringe villages complete with ponies and other denizens of the neighbouring wide open spaces. North Gorley in particular has all the right ingredients: an unfenced road and adjacent green with bordering cottages, semi-itinerant ponies and donkeys, an old thatched pub and a village pond. The pub, so I was told, was built from clay excavated opposite, thus creating the pond. And one of the ponies and one of the donkeys turn up at the pub every opening time in expectation of refreshment. It is to be hoped they are not in danger of becoming alcoholics.

Does 'Gorley' mean 'dirty clearing'? 'Ley' certainly means 'clearing', and 'gor' is Old English for 'dirt' although it could derive from 'gara', meaning 'triangular plot of ground'. On the other hand, Heywood Sumner in *Cuckoo Hill: The Book of Gorley* confidently interprets it as 'the open forest place where cattle lie'. One small point I will mention in passing is that the only real mud we had to circumvent throughout this seven-miler was along a short section of track just off the metalled road through North Gorley.

Walk 13

Distance: ***Allow 4 hours for this seven mile walk.***
Leaving The Old Beams behind you on your right, head north along the footway between A338 and a short succession of old cottages, then take care as you cross the busy highway to follow the road that heads west towards Harbridge. You immediately cross Ibsley Bridge and then turn left through a wicket-gate to follow a path across a meadow. Where the path divides the leftward spur is private. Here you bear right to follow what becomes a riverside path to the first of the many stiles you cross on this walk.

The river-edge path continues to the next stile, having crossed which you follow a clear path diverging right from the river to cross a meadow. Beyond the next

Pub facilities
Old Beams, Ibsley.
A spectacularly ancient confection of thatch and knobbly beams draws the eye of passers-by unfailingly to this free house on the east side of the busy A338, though as a pub it is not all that old. What had been just a pair of pretty cottages became a tearoom in World War II. Proceed either to the restaurant or to the main, self-service bar with its mouth-watering array of viands laid out for you to see. Weekday opening hours are 1100 (or earlier) to 1430 and 1800 to 2300, Sunday hours being as usual, and food may be ordered between 1200-1415 and 1900-2200ish seven days a week. As a popular food house this is always busy, lunchtimes and evenings. Menu items range from roast of the day, home made steak and kidney pie with vegetables and potatoes, curried beef and turkey, to rump, sirloin, fillet and T-bone steaks from best Scotch beef, turkey and bacon pie, smoked trout or mackerel, not forgetting various cold meats, ploughman's, sandwiches and hot meat roll. Real ales include Bishop's Tipple, Old Thumper, Royal Oak, Burton, Wadworth 6X, Ringwood Best Bitter and HSB. There is a rear garden, a canopied outside area and a large rear car park which pub-using walkers may use. Parties of walkers are regularly catered for.

Royal Oak, North Gorley.
Open on weekdays from 1100-1430 (until 1500 on Saturdays) and from 1800-2300 and at the usual hours on Sundays, this charming

stile carry on to a footbridge over an Avon sidestream with a stile on either side of it. Here you emerge on to a lane at the end of a metalled section where it turns right and becomes gravelled. Continue ahead along this hedged, unmetalled lane to where three dwellings including a farmhouse face a green with a reedy pond in it at the little hamlet of Turmer.

Turn right here, with the farmhouse to your left as you cross a stile to follow the left-hand edge of a pasture, with an open-sided thatched barn on your left-hand side behind the farmhouse. Beyond the next stile follow the tree-hedged leftward edge of another pasture to a further stile, beyond which you veer slightly right to cross a stile leading out on to a lane just west of Harbridge. Follow this left-handed past Kent Cottage, on your left, before crossing a stile by a footpath sign on your right.

You now follow the right-hand edge of an arable field to a stile at its far right corner. Cross this by one of the Avon's sidestreams to reach the end of a gravel lane by Cobley Cottage, to the right of it. The gravel lane leads you left-handed past scattered thatched dwellings to join a metalled lane at Harbridge Green, directly opposite a partly thatched house with a tiled gable on which is a solar panel — an uncommon blend of ancient and modern.

thatched pub on a picturesque Forest-edge byway takes orders for food between 1200-1400 and 1900-2130 seven days a week. As well as five or six daily specials, roasts, chillis, curries and items like egg and chips, toasted sandwiches and ploughman's are available. Real ales include Ringwood Best Bitter, Flower's Original and a guest ale. Guinness, lagers, cider and wines are also on draught and coffee is always available. This is a popular social centre with a flourishing darts team and is a regular venue for guest cricketers. Morris dancers and the local Hyde brass band perform periodically in summer. Facilities include a beer garden, a family and games room. A friendly ghost called Hannah lives upstrairs and is apt to be talkative. The oak which grows in front of the pub may not be royal, but is certainly ancient.

Here, as elsewhere on the route thus far and for some little way yet to come, you are on The Avon Valley Path, a 34-mile walking route from Christchurch to Salisbury. Opened in 1992, this is well-signposted throughout, with a logo in the form of a two-arched bridge to single it out from numerous intersecting paths. One of these signs here directs you right-handed to follow the road as far as a stile on your left. Cross this to follow the left-hand edge of a pasture to another stile, beyond which you head diagonally right and slightly uphill across a further pasture to a stile in a fence a few yards left of a cottage garden. Cross this to follow the arrowed route left-ahead across a grassy hump to a stile preceding a road.

Follow the road right-handed, then soon turn left by a footpath sign to cross a stile alongside a gate. You now follow a fenced gravel farm track to a stile right-ahead of you. Cross this and turn right to follow the right-hand edge of a pasture to a stile preceding a footbridge over a minor arm of the Avon. Beyond another stile your path bends left to head north across a rough pasture. Cut across the far left-hand corner of this, bearing right to another stile, beyond which you follow the right-hand edge of another weedy pasture. Bear slightly right with the pasture's alignment to cross two stiles within feet of each other. Beyond this you

Bickton Mill

follow a tree-lined, grass-centred gravelly track for a little way.

Cross the first stile on the left of this to cross rough ground to the next stile about 100 yards ahead. Cross this and continue ahead across the next pasture, veering right towards the end of it to cross a stile immediately to the right of a concrete trough. At a junction of paths just beyond this you leave The Avon Valley Path itself and turn right to bridge one of the Avon's lesser arms followed by a succession of minor sidestreams. Alongside a fish farm your path joins a track which you follow right-handed across the main river to Bickton Mill, now private residential property. Turn left to cross the mill-race and join a road which you follow right-handed through Bickton village.

Where this soon bends left and another lane bears half-right, follow the latter. As you approach where a house right-ahead of you faces the river across a lawn, turn left to follow a farm road through Bickton Farm. Leaving the farm buildings on your right, after crossing an earth barrier placed as an obstacle to unauthorised vehicles follow a gravel track ahead, with a field to your right. Where a cypress hedge soon abuts the track on your left, turn right to cross the arable field there at right-angles to your route of approach from Bickton Farm.

On the field's far side cross a stile, then cross the busy A338—take care—before crossing a stile directly ahead. Head across the arable field beyond to a point just left of a right-angled bend in the hedge left-ahead, beyond the field. You emerge through a gap here on to a lane, which you follow right-handed for a few yards before turning right by a footpath sign to enter and cross a field on a route in alignment with where the sign points. Make for a gap in the hedge on the field's far side just to the right of a slight bend in it. After passing through it keep to the same straight alignment as before. Cross a stile directly ahead to follow an arrowed route half-right across a corner of a paddock to the next stile. Cross this and head for the next stile preceding a fenced path and another stile. Skirt right-handed of a bungalow to cross a final stile preceding the next road.

This you follow right-handed through North Gorley, with its pony-haunted green, its duck-thronged pond and its Royal Oak pub, a hostelry very much in keeping with its Forest-edge surroundings. The unfenced road leads on ahead to

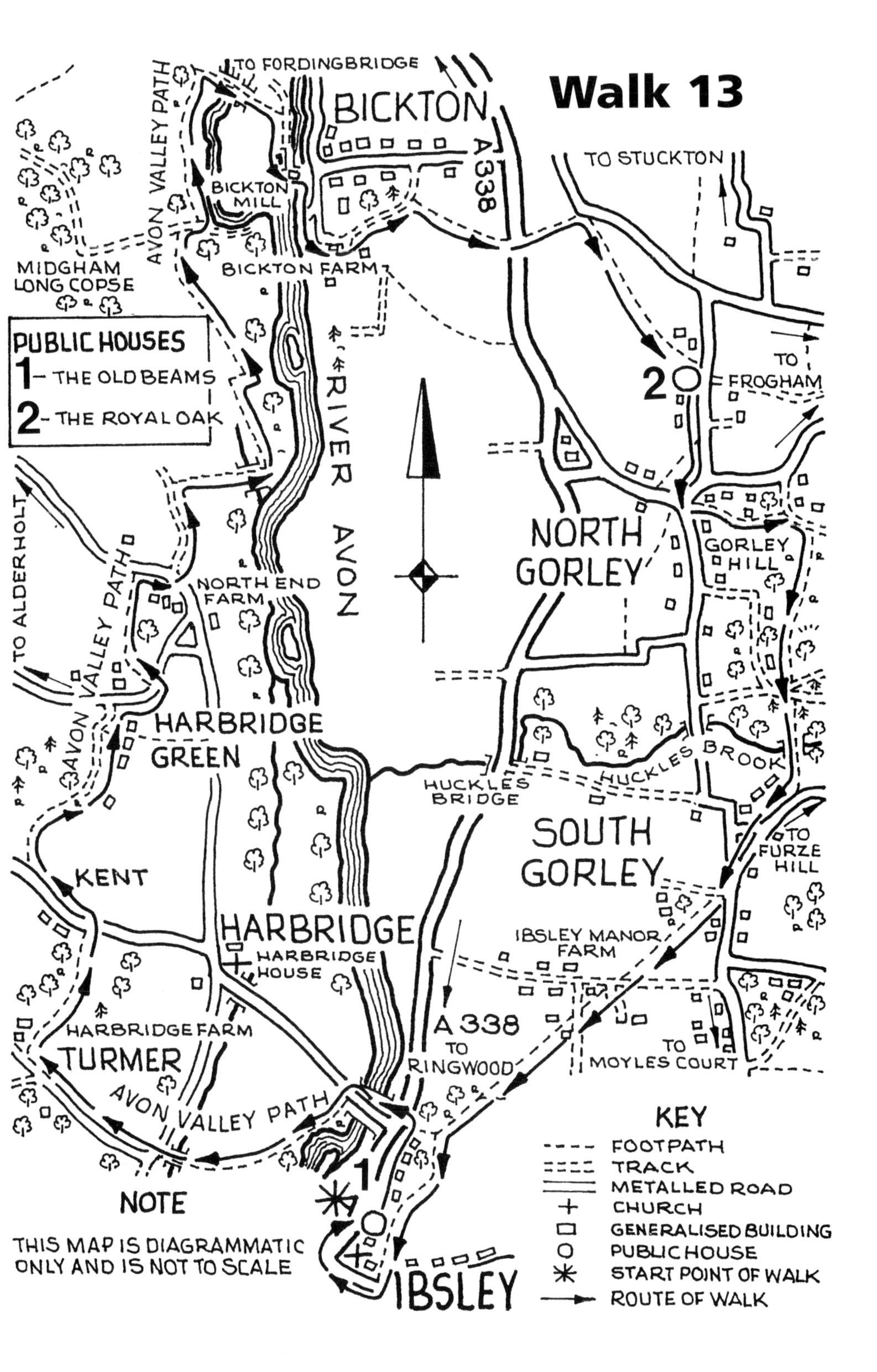

Walk 13
TO FORDINGBRIDGE
BICKTON
A 338
TO STUCKTON
AVON VALLEY PATH
BICKTON MILL
BICKTON FARM
MIDGHAM LONG COPSE
PUBLIC HOUSES
1- THE OLD BEAMS
2- THE ROYAL OAK
RIVER AVON
TO FROGHAM
TO ALDERHOLT
NORTH GORLEY
GORLEY HILL
NORTH END FARM
HARBRIDGE GREEN
HUCKLES BROOK
HUCKLES BRIDGE
SOUTH GORLEY
TO FURZE HILL
KENT
HARBRIDGE
HARBRIDGE HOUSE
IBSLEY MANOR FARM
A 338
TO RINGWOOD
TO MOYLES COURT
HARBRIDGE FARM
TURMER
AVON VALLEY PATH
NOTE
THIS MAP IS DIAGRAMMATIC ONLY AND IS NOT TO SCALE
IBSLEY
KEY
FOOTPATH
TRACK
METALLED ROAD
CHURCH
GENERALISED BUILDING
PUBLIC HOUSE
START POINT OF WALK
ROUTE OF WALK

a point just past the first leftward turning, where you turn left just past Forge Cottage to follow a rather squelchy grass track fenced from neighbouring private property. This joins a gravel lane which you follow right-ahead, climbing fairly steeply to emerge past hill-slope paddocks and a dwelling on to the crest of Gorley Hill, with Gorley Common directly ahead.

Here turn fairly sharply right-handed to follow a path through bracken and scattered trees along the hill-crest, with views of the Avon across the low ground to your right. Where the ridge path fairly soon divides, keep right-ahead, downhill, to cross a gravel track and some grass beyond. This brings you to a grass-and-gravel track preceding a stile and a fenced footpath leading downhill to another stile. Beyond this the fenced path continues between paddocks to a bridge across the Huckle Brook, one of those brown streams that flow from the New Forest's western moorlands into the Avon.

Cross a paddock directly ahead now to a stile preceding a lane which you follow right-handed to South Gorley. Where the lane forks keep left ahead to join another lane along which you continue left-ahead for a few yards to a driveway turning off to your right. Follow this before crossing a waymarked footpath stile by a bungalow immediately to your left. The next stile precedes a fenced path between gardens to another stile, beyond which you cross what we found to be a muddy corner of a nursery, left of a greenhouse, and then cross a stile directly ahead. You now cross a field to a stile preceding another field, a stile on the far side of which leads into an unmetalled lane.

Cross the lane diagonally and the stile now directly opposite to yet another stile just ahead. You now head diagonally across a paddock to a stile in the far hedge. This precedes another lane which you cross. The stile on the far side precedes a grassy area to the right of a bungalow, the right-hand edge of which you follow before crossing three stiles in quick succession. You next cross a field to a stile decidedly on the tilt in the far hedge. After crossing this head diagonally right to a hedge corner from which you continue along a hedgeline to where your own path converges with The Avon Valley Path.

If directions from the point where you left the last metalled road seem mildly confusing, all you really need remember is to follow a straight line from one field boundary-stile to another. Having joined The Avon Valley Path, cross a stile on your right to follow the path through bushes to the next stile. Cross this and follow the left-hand edge of the next pasture to where two stiles face different directions. Cross or walk round the left-hand one to follow the right-hand edge of a field as far as a stile in the right-hand hedge. Cross this to the hedgerow on the far side of the next field, through which you cross a stile on your right to follow the left-hand edge of a garden. Leaving this by another stile, you follow the left-hand edge of a paddock to a positively final stile, preceding a short driveway leading out on to a road, which you follow right-handed for a few yards to pass Ibsley's Church of St Martin on your right by your point of emergence on to A338. Directly to your right here is The Old Beams and your walk's end.

Avon Valley Paths near Fordingbridge

WALK 14
At least 4 hours
6 ½ miles
Walk begins page 85

Maps
Landranger 1:50,000
Sheets 184 and 195
Pathfinder 1:25,000
or Outdoor Leisure Map
Map Reference of Start/Finish
SU153162

How to get there
The walk starts at Lower Burgate, on the Salisbury-Ringwood road just north of Fordingbridge. From Southampton follow A3024, M271 and westbound M27 to Cadnam, B3079 to Brook and B3078 to Fordingbridge bypass, which you follow in the Salisbury direction for under a mile to Lower Burgate, where The Tudor Rose Inn is on your left. Leave Bournemouth via Wessex Way to follow A338 to its junction with A31, which you follow east for a very short distance before filtering left to resume A338, which you follow north around Fordingbridge to Lower Burgate. Wilts & Dorset buses on service X7 from Southampton via Plaitford to Salisbury connect with buses on service X3 from Salisbury to Bournemouth and Poole and vice-versa, which pass through Lower Burgate.

Background to the Walk

Pick any part of it you choose, and the Avon Valley has delights enough to lure any country lover. Now that The Avon Valley Path from Salisbury to Christchurch has been opened, walkers can enjoy this riverine region in a way not previously possible. You will encounter the long-distance route, with its bridge logo on waymarking signs at appropriate places, at several points on this circular walk, which steers clear of metalled roads for all but a small fraction of its length.

Your starting-point, Lower Burgate, is a hamlet just on the Salisbury side of Fordingbridge, with a westerly loop of the Avon sweeping right past it. Burgate House, farther south, in its own grounds adjoining a particularly scenic stretch of the river, is national headquarters of the Game Conservancy, a body devoted to propagating research into the conservation and management of pheasants, partridges, grouse and other game species. Fryern Court, another notable local residence, was the home of artist Augustus John.

Burgate itself, or at any rate Lower Burgate — Upper Burgate is a few hundred yards up the road — has some attractive timber-framed houses. The Tudor Rose Inn and The Hour Glass, nearby, occupy premises which are outstanding examples of the kind. With the noise-polluted present day right on their doorstep, these preserve more than a hint of tranquil times when wheeled traffic on what is now the busy A338 crunched its leisurely way over gravel and was dependent entirely on horsepower.

Burgate, as a placename, has an ancient ring to it. 'Burh', we are reminded, was Old English for 'fortified

Pub facilities
Tudor Rose Inn,
Lower Burgate

This eyecatching assemblage of thatch, ancient beams and whitewashed walls half-smothered in wisteria is said to date in part from the 14th century and to include an original fireplace. In recent times it has been considerably extended, so harmoniously in character with what was there before that you might never guess the difference. It has been a pub pnly since around 1970, prior to which it was a French restaurant. Owned by Devenish, it is run as a traditional pub in all respects. Opening times are 1100-1500 and 1800-2300 on summer weekdays and 1200-1430 and 1800-2300 in winter, Sundays being as usual. Guest beers are a partiular feature, brews being changed at regular intervals but Wadworth 6X, Flower's Original, Ringwood Best and Bentley's Yorkshire Bitter are usually available. Food may be ordered between 1200-1400 and 1830 (1900 on Sundays)-2100, menus rotating with the seasons. A typical summer menu may feature 5 starters, 12 main dishes and 3 different salads. Popular dishes include home made cottage pie, home made chilli and home made vegetable lasagne, all served with salad, also home cooked ham, egg, chips and salad, breaded plaice, breaded scampi, breaded seafood platter and chicken Kiev with chips, peas and salad. Other favourites are chicken breast served in a stilton and leek sauce, 8oz gammon, egg and pineapple and 8oz sirloin steak with onion rings, grilled

The Tudor Rose Inn at Lower Burgate

place'. 'Gate' was apt to mean 'goat', so was there a fortified place here where goats were kept? The combination sounds unlikely, so perhaps 'gate' meant 'gate' after all, with the hamlet being located at the gate of a fortified place. What fortified place, though? A mile away, across the river, is an ancient earthwork called Frankenbury, but surely that is a mite too distant — and indeed on the wrong side of the river.

On this walk you pass through Stuckton, whose name perhaps derives from 'Stockton', meaning 'farmstead at an adjoining hamlet' according to Mills's *Dictionary of English Place-Names*. The same authority suggests that Bickton, also on our route, perhaps means 'farmstead of a man called Bica'. Fordingbridge is less mysterious. There has apparently been a bridge across the Avon there since Saxon times, though the Romans, who came earlier, made do with a ford without a bridge. The seven-arched bridge of today was rebuilt and widened in 1841 to follow the style of its mediaeval original, on which at one time a watchman was stationed to keep an eye on all who passed and make sure the King's game or other property was not being spirited away from the New Forest.

Fordingbridge today is a compact and pleasant little town bracketing the junction of the old A338 with the road to Cranborne and Wimborne. The Church of St Mary, at its south-western end, has been largely rebuilt more than once, the predominating style being Early

English with additional influences from the Decorated and Perpendicular periods. A delightful feature of our own time is the floral carpet made by parishioners towards the end of summer every second year and laid along the full length of the central aisle. When we looked in while doing this walk a carpet of flowers from local gardens had just been completed and put in place — a superb work of art by any standards and a highly creditable achievement by the team of ladies concerned.

As is the case with Walk 13, some of the footpaths followed on this walk are liable to be flooded in winter, when the River Avon regularly overflows and inundates much of the valley.

tomatoes, chips, peas and salad, and the famous Tudor Rose mixed grill with sausage, steak, chop, gammon, egg, chips, tomatoes, mushrooms, peas and salad. Children are admitted except to the bar areas. Walkers may leave their cars in the large pub car park if they are also using the pub. The pub is said to be haunted by the ghost of a Cavalier, who makes his presence known by knocking courteously on a door and then peremptorily slamming it, a habit so disconcerting that nearly all the internal doors have been removed!

Three Lions, Stuckton
This is a small free house open between 1100-1500 and 1900-2300 from Tuesdays to Saturdays and closed on Sundays and Mondays. Freshly prepared food, most of it cooked to order, is a speciality, all pates, soups, terrines, mousses and desserts being made on the premises. The menu changes from lunch to dinner daily and is detailed on blackboards inside. Selected wines in all price brackets including half-bottles are available. Ports and dessert wines are served by the glass and customers who only require a drink are encouraged with fine real ales.

Walk 14

Distance: ***Allow four hours for this six-and-a-half mile walk.***

Take care as you cross the extremely busy A338 from The Tudor Rose Inn to follow the main road south for a few yards before turning left opposite a thatched and timber-framed cottage to follow a concreted farm road. This leads to Burgate Manor Farm. The lovely old farmhouse lies in its garden to your left as you approach the farm buildings, just beyond which you fork left where the Avon Valley Path sign at that point indicates. By what is almost certainly the only suspension footbridge in the county, the path you now follow crosses the main arm of the Avon — a very substantial body of water by Wessex standards.

'Please bolt the gate' says a notice just ahead of you here on the decrepit structure in question, but the decrepitude we found too far advanced to make this possible. A raised footpath now leads ahead across a typical valley pasture to where a twist in the path precedes a fenced footway. This crosses various concrete-bridged sidestreams of the Avon: 'runners' as these were called by the old-time 'drowners' whose job it was to adjust the sluices controlling their flow. This enabled selected pastures to be flooded in early spring, thereby becoming in the true sense watermeadows where an extra early flush of grass could thus be encouraged.

A gate with a stile alongside it precedes a grass-and-gravel lane, flanked at first by a sidestream to your right, then hedged on both sides as it rises gently away

Near Burgate on the Avon: Hampshire's only footpath suspension bridge?

from the river towards Folds Farm. This is, or was, the home of millionaire market trader Oliver Cutts, a well known local personality who began life as a Londoner and later divided his time between running a modest market stall at Salisbury and looking after a smart hotel he owned in the New Forest, where he liked to be known as 'the Master of Rhinefield'. With the black bowler hat and pinstripe suit he wore on all occasions, he was an unforgettable character.

As you approach Folds Farm, ignore the first footpath-signposted track diverging right and carry on past farm buildings to a junction of gravel lanes where another footpath sign points your way right-handed. Accessible to walkers but otherwise private, the uphill gravelled way you follow gives leftward views across a vale where the farmhouse snuggles in one corner while New Forest woodlands rise beyond. The byway's gradient fairly soon eases, and where woodland appears ahead pass through a metal gate on your right beside which a yellow waymarking arrow points out the direction now to be followed.

Heading diagonally right, you follow a fairly well-defined path across what we found as a weedy pasture, descending to a robust wooden stile on the edge of woodland, where we sheltered from a shower and enjoyed our lunchtime picnic. Crossing the stile, your path dips slightly and then climbs leftward to skirt the rim of the prehistoric earthwork called Frankenbury. Perched as this is on the edge of high ground directly above the Avon Valley, it clearly gave the far-reaching views so important to pre-Roman Britons in detecting the approach of hostile intruders.

To reach the path encompassing the earthworks we had to pick our way through the debris of the fallen limb of a beech tree which I hope will have been cleared before you tackle the walk. If you encounter any such hazards, inform the county footpath authority so that steps may be taken to rectify the problem as soon as possible.

With the earthwork to your left and a fairly steep beech-clad slope descending to your right, your well-used path curves gently left. With Frankenbury soon behind you, farmland appears to your left and you join a gravel path leading on ahead to a road which you follow through the extensive Sandy Balls Country Holiday Centre. Caravans, tents, chalets and a variety of facilities for the many

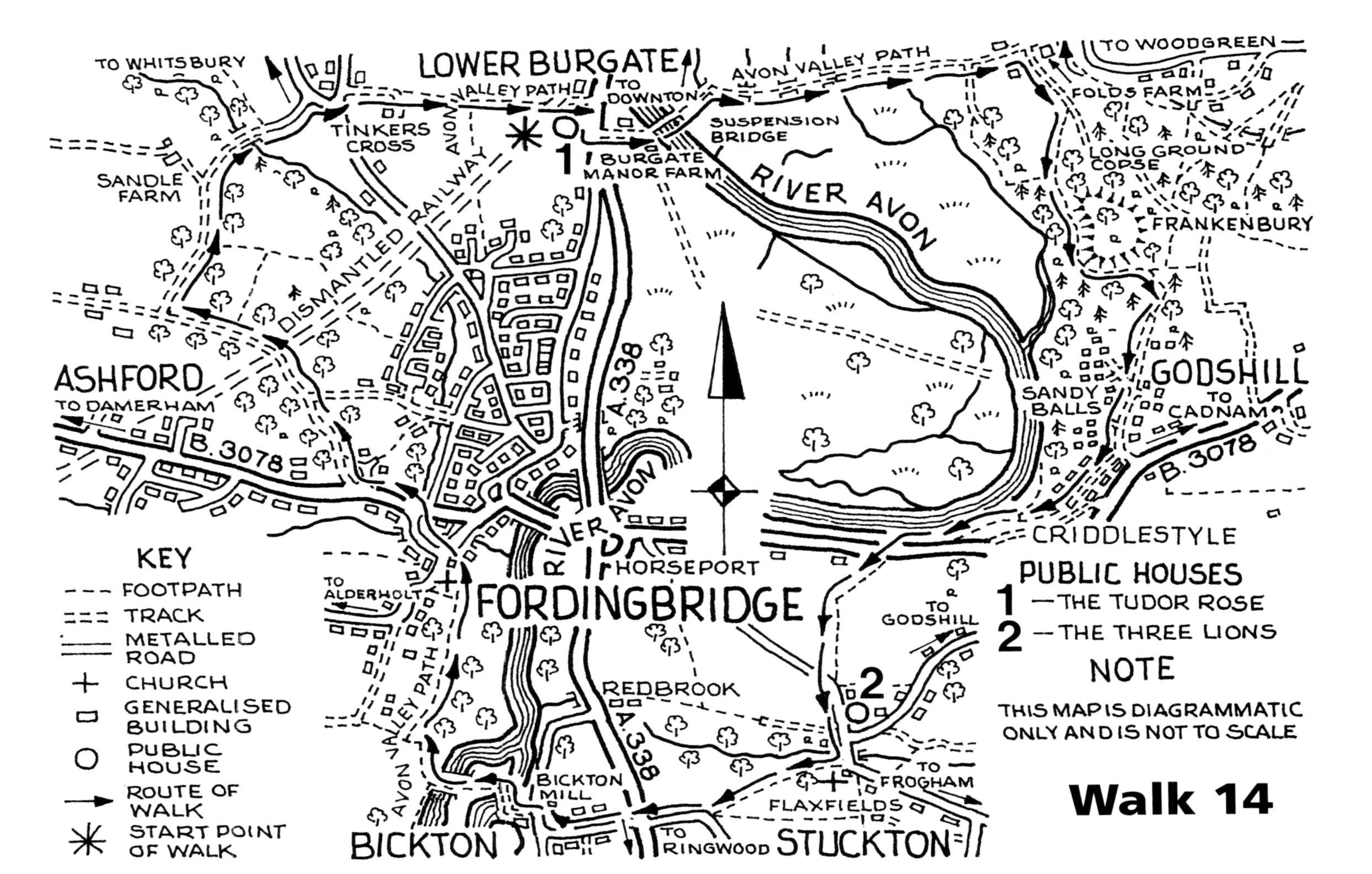

Walk 14
TO WHITSBURY
LOWER BURGATE
TO DOWNTON
AVON VALLEY PATH
TO WOODGREEN
FOLDS FARM
TINKERS CROSS
AVON
SUSPENSION BRIDGE
BURGATE MANOR FARM
LONG GROUND COPSE
SANDLE FARM
DISMANTLED RAILWAY
RIVER AVON
FRANKENBURY
ASHFORD
TO DAMERHAM
B.3078
A.338
GODSHILL
SANDY BALLS
TO CADNAM
CRIDDLESTYLE
HORSEPORT
TO ALDERHOLT
FORDINGBRIDGE
TO GODSHILL
REDBROOK
BICKTON MILL
FLAXFIELDS
TO FROGHAM
TO RINGWOOD
BICKTON
STUCKTON
KEY
FOOTPATH
TRACK
METALLED ROAD
CHURCH
GENERALISED BUILDING
PUBLIC HOUSE
ROUTE OF WALK
START POINT OF WALK
PUBLIC HOUSES
1 — THE TUDOR ROSE
2 — THE THREE LIONS
NOTE
THIS MAP IS DIAGRAMMATIC ONLY AND IS NOT TO SCALE

The Three Lions at Stuckton

vacationers who come here succeed each other as you follow the main arterial road of the complex, joined in its turn by various other roads and environed throughout by trees.

Within yards of the main entrance take a right-turning holiday-centre road which, like the road you have been following to this point, is also a public footpath. Metalled at first, the road becomes gravelled as it leads on past residential bungalows to the end of the holiday centre. An arrowed path leads on ahead downhill close to the leftward edge of the wood called Sandy Balls. As you descend steeply to a stile preceding a meadow a superb view across the Avon Valley, directly ahead, presents itself. Cross the stile, and the meadow, to a further very low stile leading out on to the Cadnam-Fordingbridge road at Criddlestyle.

Follow the road right-handed, downhill, to a stile on your left with a footpath sign alongside it. Cross the stile and head diagonally right across a meadow to a double stile at the meadow's far corner. Cross this in its turn and carry on in the same direction to a stile on the far side of the next pasture, next to the second of a series of power line posts on that side of the meadow. Having crossed this, follow the left-hand edge of the pasture beyond to the next stile, then the leftward edge of the next pasture. A stile at the end of this leads out on to a lane which you follow left-ahead through Stuckton, passing The Three Lions pub on your left.

Carry on through Stuckton, one of a series of mini-villages flanking the New Forest's western borderland and stretching south to Ringwood and beyond. After crossing a stream called Ditchend Brook turn right by a telephone kiosk to follow a streamside track and path, with Stuckton's Evangelical Church and a graveyard to your left. Beyond a decayed wicket-gate a hedged path leads away from the stream to your right and brings you soon to a stile preceding a meadow, the right-hand edge of which you follow for about 50 yards before bearing half-left and heading towards a stile two-thirds of the way along the far hedge. Cross this last-mentioned stile and head diagonally across the flat pasture beyond to its far corner, where a stile serving your own path and another path which converges from your left precedes a lane which you follow right-handed.

Not many yards ahead you cross A338 and continue along another lane into Bickton, a little Avon Valley village just far enough from the main road to preserve a measure of old-time peace and with more than a sprinkling of thatch among its dwellings. Some of the house names tell their own story: The Old Malt House, for one, and Forge Cottage for another — the village blacksmith's hammer is silent now and has been for many a year. The White House, on your left, is not one of Bickton's older dwellings — not as old, at any rate, as The Old White House directly opposite, as its name makes a point of emphasising.

When you reach a T-junction turn right, then within a matter of yards turn left by Bickton Mill, which has been modernised. The old mill-race precedes a right-turning track that bridges the Avon's main arm, which is substantial enough, we noted, to be favoured by a bird which likes fairly sizeable sheets of water, the great crested grebe. Coots and moorhens are also in evidence.

As you approach a 'private, keep out' sign, do as it says and bear left to follow a fenced path, plainly signposted. After bridging various Avon sidestreams, your path follows the left-hand edge of a pasture and joins the Avon Valley Path before reaching a stile which you cross to follow the right-hand edge of the next pasture. Where the path forks bear left, cutting across a corner of the pasture to a stile preceding a fenced path. This skirts the right-hand edge of a field to a stile under some trees, where we took shelter from a brief but heavy summer downpour.

A further stile and then another fenced footpath section brings you to St Mary's Church at Fordingbridge, where the floral carpet laid every other year had just been completed and put into position along the central aisle when we called. On each occasion the carpet has a theme appropriate to the year.

Pass right-handed of the church to leave the churchyard by its main entrance. Follow the road ahead for a short distance, then turn left along quiet West Street to join and follow left-handed Station Road. Since the Salisbury to West Moors railway was closed in the mid-'60s, only the local police station remains to make sense of the road name. Just past this outpost of law and order turn right to follow Marl Lane, which at first is scarcely more than a footpath. It widens into an unmetalled road skirting left of housing development and then heading north-west away from the town, with a country house used nowadays as a school set amid parkland to your left.

Two hundred yards or so after crossing an old railway arch turn right at a junction of gravel lanes bordered by lime trees and head north. You soon pass Sandle Farm with its pond in the foreground on your left before crossing tree-shaded Sweatfords Water. An unsuspected heron took wing when I glanced over the parapet of the bridge which spans this brook. From the point just a little way farther on where you pass a power transformer the lane becomes metalled and heads uphill to Tinkers Cross. Here you turn right at a T-junction.

At a further lane junction just ahead turn left, then almost immediately turn right to follow a hedged gravel lane with a footpath sign at the start of it. Where the second of two private driveways soon bears right the gravel ends. Carry on ahead along a hedged path which changes back into an unmetalled road as you approach Lower Burgate. When you reach the main road turn right; The Tudor Rose Inn is just ahead.

Downland Ways near Whitsbury

WALK 15
At least 3 hours
5 1/2 miles
Walk begins page 93

Background to the Walk

Whitsbury is one of those tucked-away villages which look to having been well and truly sheltered from the world's tempests almost since the beginning of time. Closer inspection, however, reveals it as the location of a substantial fortified earthwork dating from the pre-Roman period and strongly suggestive of unchronicled conflicts well before the dawn of history. It may well have been from Whitsbury Castle that native Britons engaged invading Saxons in battle at nearby Charford in an unavailing effort to hold them on the line of the Avon. Either way, the Iron Age stronghold formed one of a chain of such defences parallel with the river's course from Old Sarum southward and therefore probably delineating some sort of tribal frontier where warfare was apt to flare up at intervals.

As if to crown and confirm all this, placename pundits tell us that the name Whitsbury derives from the 12th century 'Wiccheberia', meaning 'fortified place where wych-elms grow'. This in turn derives from 'Witeberge', which rated a mention in Domesday. The village became monastic property linked with the priory at Breamore up to the time of the Dissolution. A later owner was the Earl of Shaftesbury. At one time an annual hog fair was held here. This ceased in 1825, but the village remained mainly agricultural, with most of its menfolk being employed on farms until well within living memory.

There has been a church at Whitsbury since at least the 13th century. In 1877 the then incumbent, a member of the Purvis family who were prominent in local life throughout most of the 19th century, had the church

Maps
Landranger 1:50,000
Sheet 184
Pathfinder 1:25,000
Sheets SU 01/11 & SU 02/12
Map Reference of Start/Finish
SU128188

How to get there
Whitsbury lies 3 miles north-west of the Avon Valley town of Fordingbridge. From Southampton head west along A3024, M271 and M27 to Cadnam, then follow B3079 to Brook and B3078 from there to Fordingbridge, passing under Fordingbridge bypass to follow the old main road right-handed immediately east of the town centre, directly beyond which you turn left to follow the signposted road to Whitsbury. From Bournemouth follow Wessex Way and A338 to Ringwood, briefly joining eastbound A31 before resuming A338 for Fordingbridge, where you bear left at the start of the bypass to skirt east of the town centre before turning left where the signppost points to Whitsbury. On certain days Herrington's Coaches of Alderholt, near Fordingbridge, operate buses between Fordingbridge and Salisbury to Whitsbury, en route to Rockbourne. Otherwise, bus users are advised to start the

The Cartwheel at Whitsbury

extensively restored, so that what we see today is a simple but striking brick-built structure with a tall, slim western tower and a barrel-vaulted nave. Further restorative work was undertaken in 1963. The path leading up to it from the village is so steep that old-time undertakers' men sometimes stumbled with their burdens while carrying coffins for burial services. This was remedied by the construction of a longer but much less steeply graded route to the hilltop church.

Between the church and Glebe House, which was formerly the rectory and is Whitsbury's only listed building, remains of a Roman building complete with hypocaust (or under floor heating system) have been found. Roman coins and other relics have also come to light at Whitsbury Castle, providing evidence of its use in some form subsequent to the Iron Age.

The original Whitsbury Manor House was demolished in 1826. The house so-called today is a focal point of Whitsbury Manor Stud. Horses bred and trained here include some of the most famous names in racing, Desert Orchid being among them. Racing is the lifeblood of the community today. Grazing paddocks for horses surround the village, and the gallops for which the surrounding downland is so well suited are much in evidence on this walk. For the rest, the countryside round about is a mixture of sloping arable fields broken up by belts and clumps of timber, with larger

walk at Breamore, alighting by the Bat & Ball pub there, opposite which a by-road heads west to a fork. Bear left here and at the next T-junction turn right, then almost immediately turn left to join the route as described at that point. Bus access from Southampton is via Wilts & Dorset service X7 to Salisbury and Wilts & Dorset service 38, 43 or X3 from there to Breamore. From Poole and Bournemouth Wilts & Dorset service X3 to Salisbury passes through Breamore.

Pub facilities
Cartwheel, Whitsbury.
An eyecatching blend of period beams and brickwork, this free house occupies premises which until about 1970 also included the village shop. At one time a wheelwright was based here and the wheel of a cart is embodied in a partition between two sections of the bar which, with the restaurant, now occupies almost the whole of the building's ground floor. Pub decor includes skilfully executed drawings of dogs of various breeds and pictures of horses as a reminder of the links of the village with racing. A good selection of real ales includes Wadworth 6X, Timothy Taylor Landlord, Theakston XB, Adnam's Bitter and Burton, guest ales being chosen from some 60 popular brews. A menu common to bar and restaurant offers such specials as chicken curry with rice, poppadums and accompaniments, 6oz sirloin steak garni, prawn and mushroom pasta parmagiana and 12 inch deep pan pizza with onion, tomato,

mushroom and mozzarella topping. Meat dishes range from steak and kidney pie, smoked gammon steak, roast chicken quarter and 8oz rump steak to Continental special pizza, chilli con carne, lasagne verdi and ham and mushroom pasta. Among fish dishes you can take your choice from breaded scampi, rainbow trout, swordfish steak, grilled whole plaice, seafood salad, breaded cod fillet or tuna and pineapple pizza. A good range of starters, desserts and vegetarian dishes are also available. There is a garden and children's play area. Children may eat in the pub restaurant but are not permitted in the bar area. An open fire warms the bar in winter. Walkers using the pub may leave their cars in the pub car park but are advised to arrive early to find space on Sundays especially. Pub opening hours are 1100-1430 and 1800-2300 on weekdays and as usual on Sundays. Food may be ordered between 1200-1400 and 1900-2130 but on Tuesdays is only available at lunchtime.

woodlands stretching south and east towards the Avon Valley.

In many ways the scenery is typical of south Wiltshire. Until 1895, indeed, Whitsbury was in Wiltshire. Its transfer that year to Hampshire is a reminder that alterations to county boundaries in our own time are by no means the first to have changed the shape of the ancient shires of Wessex, something of a culture shock though this is to many who live in the counties concerned.

Breamore, next door, is truly ancient. Its church was built about AD980, a date not forgotten a thousand years later when millenary celebrations included refurbishment of wall paintings from times well before the Dissolution. A striking feature of the building is the extensive use made of flints in its construction. Fully exposed to our view today, in pre-Norman times, experts tell us, they would have been covered over in plaster.

Not all of the church is of quite such great antiquity. The east doorway is typically Norman, and the chancel was largely rebuilt in the 14th century, but the long-and-short quoins of the central tower and the stonework of the south transept are among substantial relics which make this place of worship at Breamore the best-preserved Saxon church in Hampshire. Another feature of special note is the Saxon stone rood above the nave doorway, depicting Christ with the Virgin Mary and St John. This has been badly mutilated, probably under instructions from Bishop Robert Horne of Winchester not many years after the Dissolution.

The pre-Reformation church was associated with Breamore Priory, situated alongside the Avon a little way north of Breamore Mill. The surrounding watermeadows have been maintained as such for centuries, but when the priory was first established as a house of the Austin canons during the reign of Henry I, this flat land may still have retained the character of the broomy moor or marsh which first gave rise to the name of Breamore.

Following the Dissolution in 1536, the manor of Breamore and another manor were given to Henry, Marquess of Exeter, a grandson of Edward IV. He was not to enjoy his good fortune for long. Just two years later Henry VIII, suspecting the marquess as having designs on the throne, had his head cut off. A later owner was William Doddington, Treasurer to Elizabeth I, who in 1583 built that far-famed specimen of Elizabethan architecture, Breamore House. Backed by extensive

The Breamore Mizmaze

hilltop woodland and flanked by beautifully timbered parkland which slopes gently down to the half-mile distant A338 and the Avon Valley, the mansion has been home to many generations of Hulses. It is opened to the public, while another estate attraction is a countryside museum with exhibits highlighting various aspects of rural life as lived in the past.

At one time clustered about the church, which lies just in front of Breamore House, the present-day village of Breamore largely dates from the 17th century and has its centre on the main road. Its mellow cottages of warm brick with their characteristic leadlight windows have that unity of style which confirms common origin and ownership as homes for those whose livelihoods were linked with the local 'big house' and with the estate of which Breamore continues to form part. Let no one hear you call it 'Bree-moor'. 'Bremmer' is how the locals pronounce it, and so, apparently, have their forebears ever since the days of the Saxons.

Between Whitsbury and Breamore are two other notable antiquities. Giant's Grave, on Breamore Down, is a prehistoric long barrow 60 yds in length and 28 yds wide at its wider end. It has been damaged by cultivation. Better preserved is the Mizmaze, hidden away in a hilltop yew grove and protected from casual wear and tear by a fence and a cautionary notice requesting visitors just to look but not to walk on its fragile turf. The notice describes it as prehistoric. Its significance is unknown and it is scheduled now as a nationally important site as recognised by the Ancient Monuments and Archaeological Areas Act of 1979. You will see it on this walk along with a wealth of delightful scenery.

Walk 15

Distance: ***Allow three hours for this five-and-a-half mile walk.***
Leave The Cartwheel pub at Whitsbury behind you on your left as you head south-east along the village road for a few yards before turning left to follow a fenced path steeply uphill to a latched gate. Cross the rising pasture beyond this, making a bee-line for the church at the top of the hill ahead of you. A second latched gate precedes the churchyard. The church, with its latticed nave windows and its plain,

whitewashed interior projecting an image of pleasing simplicity, is normally open to visitors. We found it filled with flowers in readiness for a village wedding.

From the nave door follow a path right-handed around the rear of the building and out through a gate to follow left-handed a grass-centred gravel track. Hedged on your left and flanked by racehorse paddocks on your right, this fairly soon joins a metalled driveway which you follow ahead downhill to re-emerge on to the village road. Follow this right-handed, then turn right through a gate where a footpath sign points the way past the buildings of Whitsbury Manor Stud. Outbuildings include thatched barns with beams both vertically and diagonally — fine-looking structures indeed these are.

At the end of the buildings turn right to skirt the stud and follow a view-commanding track of grass and chalk, with a fence on your left and Whitsbury Castle's triple ramparts mantled in woodland to your right. Whitsbury Manor Farm lies to your left as you descend towards a vale beyond which cereal-growing downland is patterned with strips and tufts of timber.

At the valley bottom cross a broad, grassy drove and a stile on the other side of it to follow a footpath along the right-hand edge of arable land on rising ground, with a hedgerow to your right. You soon skirt right-handed of the southern end of a small wood of yews and beeches, then follow a track straight on through it to skirt a stile and what we found as an open gate. Carry on ahead uphill along the right-hand edge of a field, with a fence to your right.

This brings you to a stile beyond which your path joins a green lane at the southern extremity of a conifer plantation, with the Avon Valley now in view away to your right. Follow the green lane right-handed, then, where it soon forks, you bear right to climb to the edge of the grove of yews which masks the Mizmaze. Carry on along the woodland margin and then bear right at a second fork with a white notice-board in view a few yards to your right. This marks the entry point for the path leading through the yew grove to the Mizmaze, occupying a circular site with alternating shallow chalk trenches and turfy pathways forming a pattern which, from the outside, does not look unduly difficult to fathom and work out how to reach the centre. As already indicated, you are asked not to attempt this except as a mental exercise.

Walk out through the yews the way you came in and then bear right to follow a downhill path which rejoins the green lane you left after briefly following it from the southern end of the conifer plantation. Follow this right-ahead, uphill between trees and shrubs, into the old beeches and oaks of Breamore Wood. A chalk-and-gravel track leads on through this, with numerous turnings-off discreetly signposted as 'private'.

A descent of several hundred yards precedes the point where you leave the wood to skirt an expanse of parkland and pass within yards of Breamore House before continuing downhill along what is now a metalled drive to where a side path to your left leads to the Saxon church at Breamore. Spare time for at least a peep at this before returning to the main driveway and continuing downhill.

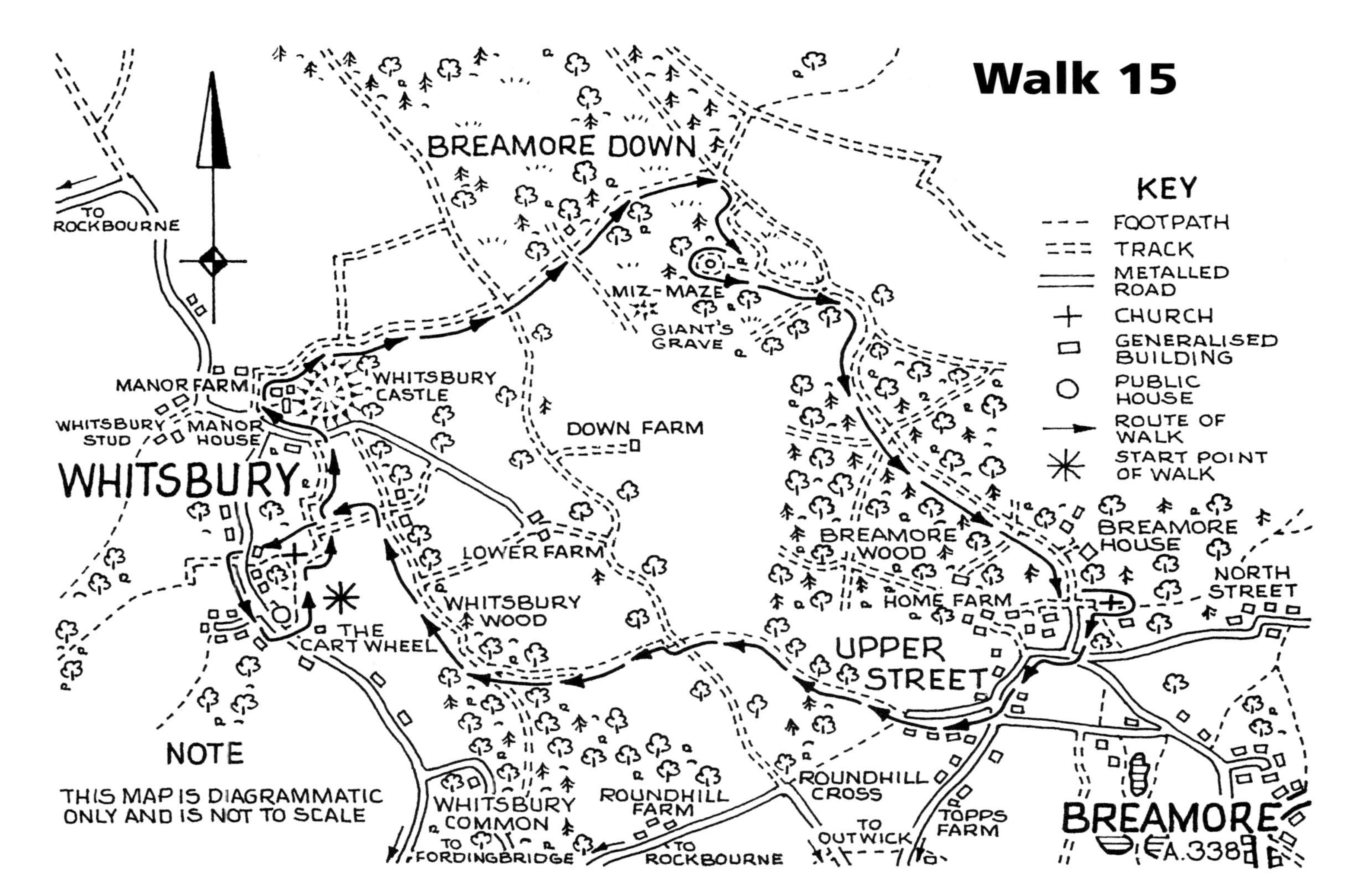

Walk 15
KEY
FOOTPATH
TRACK
METALLED ROAD
CHURCH
GENERALISED BUILDING
PUBLIC HOUSE
ROUTE OF WALK
START POINT OF WALK
TO ROCKBOURNE
BREAMORE DOWN
MIZ-MAZE
GIANT'S GRAVE
MANOR FARM
WHITSBURY CASTLE
WHITSBURY STUD
MANOR HOUSE
DOWN FARM
WHITSBURY
LOWER FARM
BREAMORE WOOD
BREAMORE HOUSE
NORTH STREET
HOME FARM
WHITSBURY WOOD
THE CART WHEEL
UPPER STREET
NOTE
THIS MAP IS DIAGRAMMATIC ONLY AND IS NOT TO SCALE
WHITSBURY COMMON
TO FORDINGBRIDGE
ROUNDHILL FARM
TO ROCKBOURNE
ROUNDHILL CROSS
TO OUTWICK
TOPPS FARM
BREAMORE
A.338

Whitsbury's hilltop church

Unless the countryside museum and adjacent tearooms are on your personal itinerary, ignore the right-hand turning to these and carry on to the next road crossing.

Turn right here to follow a lane from which two driveways bear right at a bend where you turn left. Following the public road, you head past the houses of Upper Street, an outlying part of Breamore proper. Eyecatching period dwellings are half-screened by mellow old walls as you approach the next lane turning. Here you turn right to follow a cottage-flanked cul-de-sac. Where dwellings soon end, so does the metalled road, and you continue along a tree-lined track which soon becomes a mere path hemmed in by burgeoning vegetation.

This ends at a stile, which you cross to follow a footpath downhill along the left-hand edge of farmland, with a hedge and an ancient hollow lane, now largely weed-filled, just to your left. At a valley bottom which you soon reach you pass through a gate to cross an unmetalled farm road. Pass through a double gate on the far side of this to follow a rising footpath along the right-hand edge of arable ground, with a wood on the high ground ahead. Your footpath carries on into this wood, where diverging rides are clearly marked 'private'.

Fairly soon reaching the wood's far side, carry on just within it for a few hundred yards with horse paddocks to your left. When you reach a bungalow on your right turn left to follow a railed green path between two paddocks. This leads to a T-junction of fenced paths where you turn left for Whitsbury church, heading right-handed through the churchyard to follow another fenced path which winds steeply downhill to reach the village road. Follow this left-handed to retrieve your

Wiltshire Chalk near Charlton All Saints

WALK 16
At least 3 hours
6 $^{1}/_{2}$ miles
Walk begins page 99

Background to the Walk

Charlton, experts remind us, is one of England's commoner placenames, there being no fewer than three in Wiltshire alone. With one or two exceptions, its first syllable derives from the Old English 'ceorl', meaning 'freeman', 'peasant' or 'person of low birth' — whence the modern word 'churl', which has come to signify a boorish, ill-bred, cross-grained or niggardly person! The plural is 'ceorla', and 'tun' means 'farmstead', so the name Charlton may be interpreted as 'farmstead of the freemen or peasants'.

Charlton All Saints is the full name of this quiet mini-village on the banks of the River Avon, reached by lanes which lead nowhere else but linked by footpaths with Bodenham, Downton and elsewhere in the vicinity. It lies on The Avon Valley Path, a walking route which follows the river valley south from Salisbury, and is overlooked from both east and west by the rolling south Wiltshire chalkland, much of which was at one time common grazing land for sheep. There are still some sheep on these downs but the growing of cereals is now the main agricultural activity. The New Forest is not far away — a mere three miles in a south-easterly direction — and can be clearly seen from high ground to the west in the course of this walk.

Prominent on this high ground, crowning Clearbury Down, less than two miles away, is Clearbury Ring, where mantling woodland hides the earthworks of a substantial Iron Age hill fort. You will skirt this on the walk and, looking east, you will see peeping out from the trees beyond the Avon Trafalgar House, built as Standlynch House in 1733 and renamed after the fa-

Maps
Landranger 1:50,000
Sheet 184
Pathfinder 1:25,000
Sheet SU 02/12
Map Reference of Start/Finish
SU169240

How to get there
The Stag at Charlton lies on the east side of A338, the Salisbury-Ringwood road, about 4 miles south-east of Salisbury and 1 $^{1}/_{2}$ miles north of Downton, which can be reached from Southampton via A33024, M271, westbound M27 to Cadnam, B3079 to Brook, B3078 to Bramshaw Telegraph and then B3080 via Redlynch. From Bournemouth follow A338 to its junction with A31 at Ringwood and then north, bypassing Fordingbridge and skirting the western end of Downton. Wilts & Dorset buses on service X7 from Southampton via Totton connect at Salisbury with buses on services 38, 43, 44, 45 and X3 which all pass The Stag en route to various destinations. Walkers starting from Bournemouth can travel direct to The Stag by Wilts & Dorset buses on service X3 via Ringwood and Fordingbridge.

Pub Facilities
The Stag
This Courage pub is an ideal stopping-off point for travellers on the Avon Valley main road between Salisbury, Ringwood and Bournemouth. Originally an estate house built about 200 years ago, it has a south-facing, sunny aspect and is a nice, bright pub attracting a clientele from many miles around as well as a busy passing trade. Popular brews include John Smith Bitter, Ruddles' Best Bitter and Triple Crown. Strongbow draught cider is also available in what is pre-eminently a food pub catering for families and children, for whom there is a trampoline and a climbing frame in the garden. The lunch menu offers items such as Cornish pastie, half a roast chicken, home-made shepherd's pie and steak and kidney pie, ham, egg and chips, gammon steak with egg or pineapple, 8oz sirloin steak garni, chicken curry and southern fried chicken, not forgetting three vegetarian dishes, five fish dishes and a choice of four ploughman's. Salads, sandwiches, sweets, ice cream and a special children's menu are also available. Specials when I called included chicken cordon bleu (filled with ham and cheese) and home-made tuna quiche, plus lemon sorbet, hot chocolate fudge cake and lemon tart with ice cream. Food may be ordered between 1200-1400 and 1830 (1900 Sundays)-2130. Pub opening hours are 1100 until late afternoon, 1800-2300, and as usual on Sundays. Walkers using the pub are welcome to use the large pub car park.

The Stag at Charlton All Saints

mous battle when presented by the nation to Nelson's heirs, who lived here until the present century.

Most of the land hereabouts forms part of the Earl of Radnor's Longford Castle estate. Longford Castle itself lies in a 250-acre park alongside the Avon and is a triangular house of 16th century origin. It was built by Sir Thomas Gorges, who ran out of money before it was finished. The day was saved when one of the ships of the Spanish Armada ran aground on coastal property belonging to Sir Thomas. His wife, a lady-in-waiting to Queen Elizabeth I, petitioned the monarch to allow her husband to take possession of the wreck. This turned out to be laden with treasure which amply restored Sir Thomas's fortune.

This walk covers two entirely different types of country. All but the final two miles explores the broad tract of virtually uninhabited downland stretching west from A338 just north of Downton to meet A354, the Salisbury-Blandford road, south of Coombe Bissett. This hilly land of wide open spaces is not only largely unpeopled but almost devoid of metalled roads, which makes it a region of rare serenity, with only the rumble of a tractor or two or the dust-disturbing passage of some farmer's or gamekeeper's Land-Rover to intrude on the rural quiet. Here, indeed, is a land where you can truly walk in peace, at one with nature, or such part of it as agricultural man has harmonised with his own interests: a not ungenerous portion, you are likely to agree. Leaving the high ground for the valley, you traverse field paths around Charlton, a country community all the more special for being 'on the road to nowhere' and therefore having to be sought out by those from outside who would like to know more about it.

Unpeopled chalkland west of Charlton

Walk 16

Distance: ***Allow 3 hours for this walk of about six-and-a-half miles.***
Opposite the turning for Charlton next to The Stag you follow a hedged, metalled lane heading west towards the downs on that side of A338. Within a few hundred yards roadmetal ends where the made-up road turns right at the entrance to Charlton Manor Farm, and you will not see tarmac again until towards the end of the walk when you rejoin and cross the Avon Valley highway a mile farther north. Continue along a gravel byway, rising gently and curving left-handed as you follow a dry valley bottom, with a wooded bank to your left.

Leaving the valley, the byway soon becomes grassy rather than gravelled as you continue a steady ascent to where Warren Plantation lies to your left. All the way towards this isolated hillside wood the view to your right is dominated by Clearbury Ring with its topnotch of trees, here less than a mile distant. Your grass track, as it now is, winds on and up past cattle-grazed slopes and corn-growing expanses to skirt the next pocket-handkerchief woodland, Charlton Furze, on your right-hand side.

These scattered boscages do much to enhance the scenic charm of the chalkland, breaking up, as they do, the pattern of otherwise endless undulations of mainly cereal-growing country: refreshingly spacious and uncluttered by extraneous visual elements but all the better for a modest admixture, as here, of timbered verdure. Carry on to the end of Charlton Furze, where you emerge through a gateway to join a gravel road at the most distant point of this walk from where you started, now almost three miles below and behind you. Here, on these broad and breezy uplands, we used a wayside horse-jumping trestle as a seat for our picnic lunch while enjoying the peace of our surroundings. We also relished the easterly view across the valley from which we had climbed, where tree-fringed fields beyond the Avon mingled with woods away to the south, with farmland and forest coming together on the Fordingbridge side of Downton.

Having joined the gravel road, follow its wide, straight course right-handed, north-east, with the beeches and conifers of Charlton Furze still to your right. To your rear the view is bounded by the distant green ridge of Martin Down, on the Hampshire-Dorset border, as you climb gently for half-a-mile before descending past a small wood on your left to a right-hand gate with a bridleway sign. Pass through this gateway to follow a grass track, hedged to your left but unfenced on your right, which continues north-east with Clearbury Ring now directly in front of you, presenting an ever more dramatic view beyond trees in a valley ahead as you draw closer.

Wayside travellers camped on the chalk

After crossing a stile next to a wooden gate, flanked in its turn by a metal gate, you follow a path past a belt of scrub and across what we found as a downland pasture dancing with butterflies of many hues on a bright, warm day in summer. You now rise to the edge of Clearbury Ring, which you follow right-handed to a gate and stile at the south-east end of the wooded earthwork. From here we crossed the outer ditch to mount and circumnavigate the rim of the hill fort itself, now mantled in a luxuriant growth of beech, ash and sycamore, which also covers the central area enclosed within the earthwork.

From the gate and stile last mentioned, carry on along the grass track around the outer edge of Clearbury Ring to a point directly opposite where you reached its periphery. Here your track turns away from it to head for the Avon Valley, now spread before you with Pepperbox Hill in view in the background, while beyond a left-hand hedge the spire of Salisbury Cathedral looms in the middle-distance. A quarter-of-a-mile downhill the well-defined track angles slightly right. You follow a lesser track left-handed to the near side of a gate, where you turn right to follow the left-hand edge of an arable field, with a hedge to your left.

After descending for half-a-mile you join and follow ahead part of The Avon Valley Path, a long distance walking route from Salisbury opened in 1992 as a means of exploring the river valley while avoiding roads as far as possible. This leads on down to a gateway where you cross A338. After crossing two stiles on the main road's far side you head diagonally right across a pasture towards a gate at its far corner, through which you pass to join and follow right-handed a dark and narrow tree-lined lane.

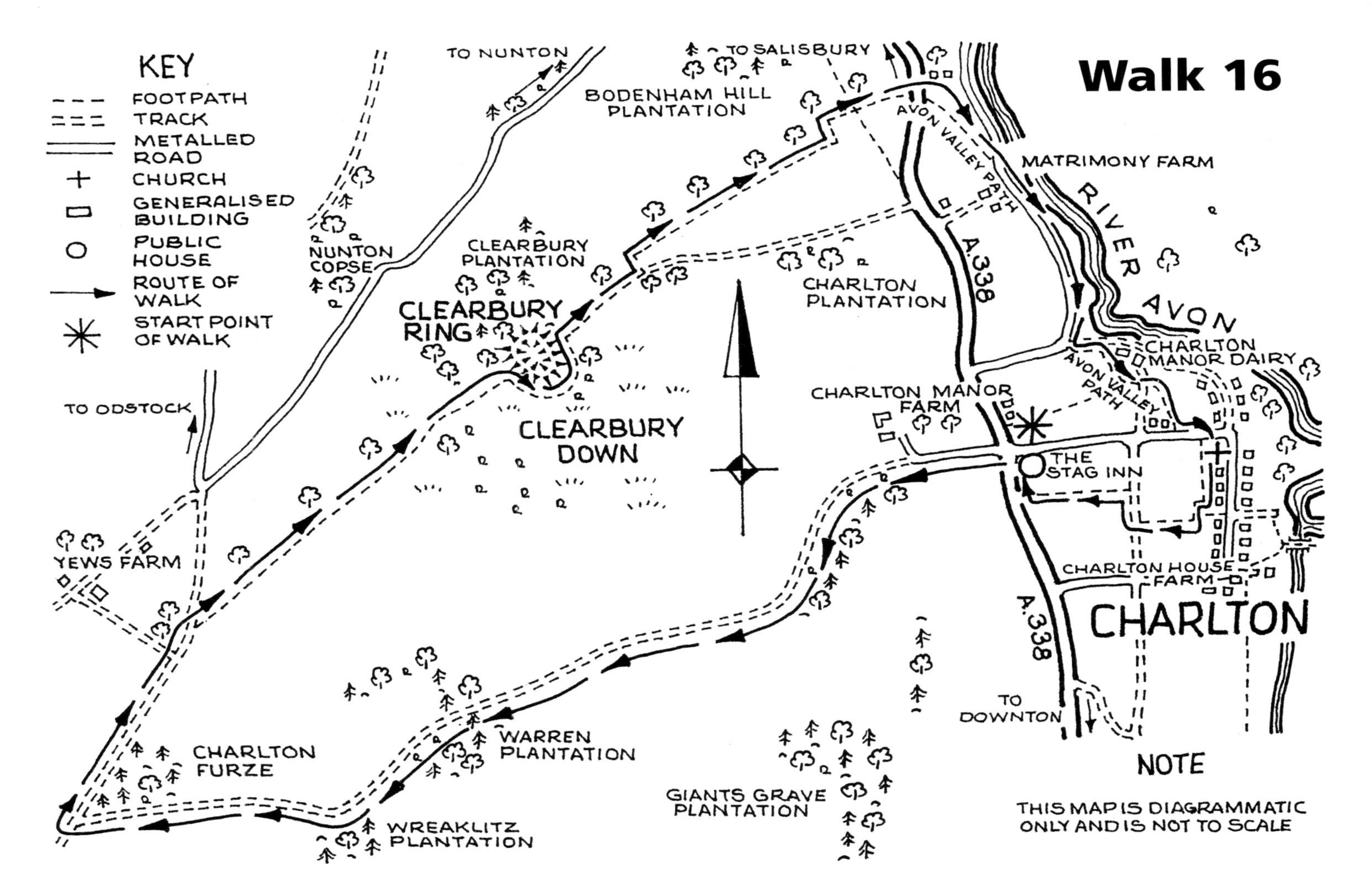
Walk 16
KEY
FOOTPATH
TRACK
METALLED ROAD
CHURCH
GENERALISED BUILDING
PUBLIC HOUSE
ROUTE OF WALK
START POINT OF WALK
TO NUNTON
TO SALISBURY
BODENHAM HILL PLANTATION
AVON VALLEY PATH
MATRIMONY FARM
RIVER AVON
NUNTON COPSE
CLEARBURY PLANTATION
CLEARBURY RING
A.338
CHARLTON PLANTATION
CHARLTON MANOR DAIRY
TO ODSTOCK
CLEARBURY DOWN
CHARLTON MANOR FARM
AVON VALLEY PATH
THE STAG INN
YEWS FARM
CHARLTON HOUSE FARM
CHARLTON
A.338
TO DOWNTON
CHARLTON FURZE
WARREN PLANTATION
GIANTS GRAVE PLANTATION
WREAKLITZ PLANTATION
NOTE
THIS MAP IS DIAGRAMMATIC ONLY AND IS NOT TO SCALE

Clearbury Ring rounds off many a view

This passes Matrimony Farm about a quarter-of-a-mile before bending right, at which point you cross a stile left-ahead of you to follow a fenced footpath, hedged on your right, with a concrete farm road to your left. Where the fenced path ends cross a stile and head diagonally across the meadow beyond to a further stile at its far corner. Cross this to follow another fenced path, hedged on your left this time, to the next stile, after crossing which you follow a muddy lane for a few yards to where this bends right. Go through a kissing-gate ahead to continue along the signposted Avon Valley Path. This heads diagonally away from the right-hand edge of the field beyond to reach a stile to the left of some cottages.

Cross the stile to follow the lane beyond left-handed to where a gate on your right precedes a path across Charlton churchyard. The modest, brick-built structure of bell-turreted All Saints Church, erected in 1851, lies to your left here and the door was locked when we passed. Pass through a further gate to follow a fenced path ahead, with Charlton's cottages to your left. When you come to a T-junction of footpaths cross a stile on your right to follow the left-hand edge of a pasture to a further stile preceding a hedged, muddy lane. Follow this lane right-handed to a somewhat rickety stile a few yards along on your left, which you cross to follow the left-hand edge of a meadow to another stile leading out on to A338. A bordering paved footpath leads right-handed for the few remaining yards to where you started. I hope you have planned your walk to arrive at a time when The Stag will be open.

A Wiltshire Walk from Whaddon

WALK 17
Allow 2 or 3 hrs
3 or 5 $1/2$ miles
Walk begins page 105

Background to the Walk

This walk starts under the lee of the chalk which rises east of the Avon Valley, south of Salisbury, to form a ridge extending from Pepperbox Hill along the length of Dean Hill and terminating just inside Hampshire. Whether the full circuit or the shorter version is opted for, the combination of hill and vale, with the extensive views that go with this, make the route a highly scenic one.

Whaddon, where the walk begins, was recorded in Domesday Book as 'Watedene', meaning 'valley where wheat is grown'. Plenty of wheat is still grown in the area, mainly, however, on the chalk, much of the valley land now being pasture. A certain amount of woodland survives from the old Royal Forest of Clarendon, which played an important part in the history of this corner of south-east Wiltshire. As a plaque in The Three Crowns pub reminds us, between the reign of Henry I and that of Richard III, Clarendon Palace some three miles to the north, was an important royal residence where kings and their courtiers came to hunt. It also served as a place of confinement when in 1357, following the Battle of Poitiers, defeated King John II of France was brought here as a prisoner by King Edward III of England, who also held captive until his release that year King David II of Scotland — a combination of circumstances preserved in memory by the name of the Whaddon hostelry.

Clarendon Palace today is a ruin which may be visited by appointment with the owners of the Clarendon estate, on which it lies. This is one of two large landed properties in Whaddon's immediate

Maps
Landranger 1:50,000
Sheet 184
Pathfinder 1:25,000
Sheets SU 02/12 & SU 22/32
Map Reference of Start/Finish SU197260

How to get there
From Southampton follow A3024, M271, westbound M27 and then A36 into Wiltshire. Nearly 1 mile beyond Pepperbox Hill fork left-ahead as if for Alderbury and within about 100 yards turn left into the car park of The Three Crowns at Whaddon. Leave Bournemouth via Wessex Way to follow A338, eastbound A31 briefly, then A338 again to Salisbury Ring Road (Churchill Way), from which turn right to follow Southampton-signposted A36. Bear right from this at the first turn-off for Alderbury, through which carry straight on to adjacent Whaddon, where The Three Crowns lies well back from the road on your right. Wilts & Dorset buses on service X7 between Southampton and Salisbury pass through Whaddon. Wilts & Dorset buses on service X3 from Poole and Bournemouth connect at Salisbury with service X7 for Southampton, passing through Whaddon.

Pub facilities
Three Crowns
Facing a section of the old main road between Southampton and Salisbury which was bypassed decades ago, and backing on to a successor highway which has been bypassed in its turn, this hostelry claims links with a time when crowned heads from three countries were present in the neighbourhood — and may actually have been guests here. Beams, ancient brickwork and a welcoming log fire in the cooler months highlight the character of a pub where traditional hospitality is the order of the day. Morland brews can be sampled here. Their real ales include Speckled Hen (a strong beer), Old Masters and hand drawn Morland Original. Ringwood Bitter, Foster's and Stella Artois lagers and Thatcher's cider are also on draught. A generous bar menu includes soup, pate, prawn cocktail, plaice, scampi, omelettes, grills, chicken Kiev, half racks of ribs, 8oz sirloin steak, toasties, burgers, filled jacket potatoes, salads, sandwiches and four types of ploughman's. Roast beef and Yorkshire pudding with onion gravy and fresh vegetables, preceded by soup, pate or fruit juice and followed by apple pie with cream attract many for Sunday lunch here. Among additional items on the separate restaurant menu (evenings only) are breaded mushrooms, dim sum, curried prawns, poached trout with orange sauce, fillet of wild Scotch salmon with Hollandaise sauce, barbecued spare ribs, gammon steak, 10oz sirloin steak, 14oz club steak, 10oz fillet steak and

neighbourhood, the other being the Longford Castle estate of the Earl of Radnor. Much of the ground covered on this walk is Longford Castle property.

Whaddon and Alderbury are virtually one community. The latter is so much the larger that it dominates its neighbour, the separate identity of which is apt to be overlooked by those who are unfamiliar with the area. Alderbury, too, has become a backwater half-forgotten by the great wide world beyond now that through traffic on the A36 has been diverted around it — much to the satisfaction, no doubt, of local people intent on enjoying a peaceful life unmarred by cars and heavy transport constantly racing past their doors. Also departed is the railway that once branched off at Alderbury to follow the Avon Valley south by way of Downton and Fordingbridge, eventually joining the old Southampton-Dorchester main line at West Moors. One of the victims of the axe wielded by Dr Beeching in the '60s, its past existence is a fact of which abundant visual evidence remains on the route of this walk, although at Whaddon, through which it once passed, almost all signs of it have vanished.

Vanished too is the village of Standlynch, once a prosperous community located in what now is open country about halfway between Whaddon and Downton. Changing patterns of rural life were the cause of its disappearance, though there is still a Standlynch Down, the foot of which you skirt on the longer version of this walk.

Walk 17

16oz T-bone steak plus a selection of desserts. Pool and darts may be played in the separate games room and there is a large family garden with many amusements for children including swings, a seesaw, climbing frames and wendy houses. Children may be brought into the restaurant. Walkers may use the large pub car park or the section of old road flanking the pub. Opening hours are 1100-1430 (until 1500 Fridays and Saturdays) and 1800-2300 on weekdays and as usual on Sundays. Food may be ordered between 1200-1400 and from 1800 (1900 Sundays) to 2100.

Distance: ***Allow 2 hours for the three mile version, 3 hours for the full five-and-a-half mile walk.***

From the south side of The Three Crowns follow the stub of the old road on that side of the pub in a westerly direction, around a metal gate across it on that side. The scrub-bordered remnants of this road lead to a metalled footpath which leads out on to the slip road from the A36 into Alderbury. Follow this ahead for a few yards, then, almost opposite a newsagent's shop, turn left to follow a badly-surfaced side road.

Flanked by dwellings, this bends right at its junction with a farm road, signposted 'Pack Path', which you ignore. Carry on to where your road splits into three and turn sharp left to follow a track misleadingly signposted 'no right of way'. This promptly becomes a narrow but well-defined public footpath, leading ahead at first and then angling right through rough pastureland and scrub to the remnants of two old stiles. Cross the field now ahead of you, veering left through it to a further stile, beyond which you follow an unmetalled road right-handed.

After passing Rectory Farm at Alderbury on your left this road soon bends right at a point from which you follow a hedged and fenced path straight ahead. This curves right and then left to reach a stile, after crossing which you follow a path that veers left through a field, with trees on your left. Beyond a further stile you cross the meadow ahead, about halfway across which another stile gave access over electric stock fencing dividing the pasture into two when I did this walk.

At this meadow's far side cross another stile to follow the right-hand edge of the meadow directly beyond, at the end of which a swing-gate precedes a hedged grass-and-gravel track which you follow left-handed. This leads into a metalled road which you follow left-handed in its turn, with the Avon Valley's level pastures spreading to your right and hedged chalk downland rising beyond. The tree-capped knoll most prominent as you look across the valley is Clearbury Ring, an Iron Age hill fort which dominates the landscape on that side at almost all stages of the walk from this point onward.

Carry on past farm buildings on your left, ignoring the track which turns left just past these, and stay on the lightly-used road until you reach the far end of the first wood on your left. This is where you turn left to follow a gated gravel road, with arable farmland to your right and oaks and hazels to your left. This wood I found pleasant if less than idyllic, thanks to a corner of it having been commandeered as a storage dump for metal skips of the kind used for transporting rubble.

At the far end of the field leave the gravel road and turn right to follow a well-defined field-edge bridleway, with a strip of woodland on your left. Where another wood soon confronts you the bridleway leads left-handed through it, with a timbered hillside to your right. A horse-jumping trestle at the wood end offered a seat for lunchtime sandwiches before I continued ahead through beech trees, then along a field-edge path with a hedgerow to my left, Pepperbox Hill looming not far ahead and arable downland extending towards the skyline on my right.

Your route runs parallel with this former railway

My map indicates a bridleway branching right-handed across this downland to converge on the next hump of high ground with the course of the old Salisbury-West Moors railway, the earthworks of which are now plainly visible. I dutifully followed the route thus suggested, but found no trace of current use as a right of way across the ploughland. Exploring further, I soon discovered that the bridleway has moved to the far side of the fields in question.

If you prefer the three-mile walk, all this is immaterial, for all you have to do is to keep straight on along the field-edge bridleway after leaving the wood. This brings you to a gate beyond which you cross a former railway arch to follow a track along the right-hand edge of the field directly beyond. At the top of the next ridge of high ground you then turn left to head back to Whaddon along an unfenced grassy track with arable farmland on both sides.

Time and energy permitting, I very strongly recommend the longer walk, if only for the sake of the views to be enjoyed along parts of it. To follow it, on the near side of the gate preceding the bridge across the old railway, turn right to follow a well-used bridle-track alongside the earthworks of the old line. This is the current route of the bridleway which formerly crossed the farmland a little way west, as already mentioned. It heads downhill to cross a metalled farm road alongside an arch where this goes under the old railway. You then continue ahead, uphill, and then gently down to another horse-jumping trestle flanked by a gate, through which you enter the next field to follow its leftward edge straight on.

A well-defined track leads you to a metal gate preceding the grounds of a farm cottage, beyond which an open gateway leads out on to a tree-bordered metalled lane. Turn left to follow this lane over the old railway's tree-lined course. Now heading east under tall horse chestnuts, you soon emerge into the open and climb gently towards where sycamores and beeches cast their shadows across the tarmac. Directly beyond a lodge-type bungalow on your right the metalled lane

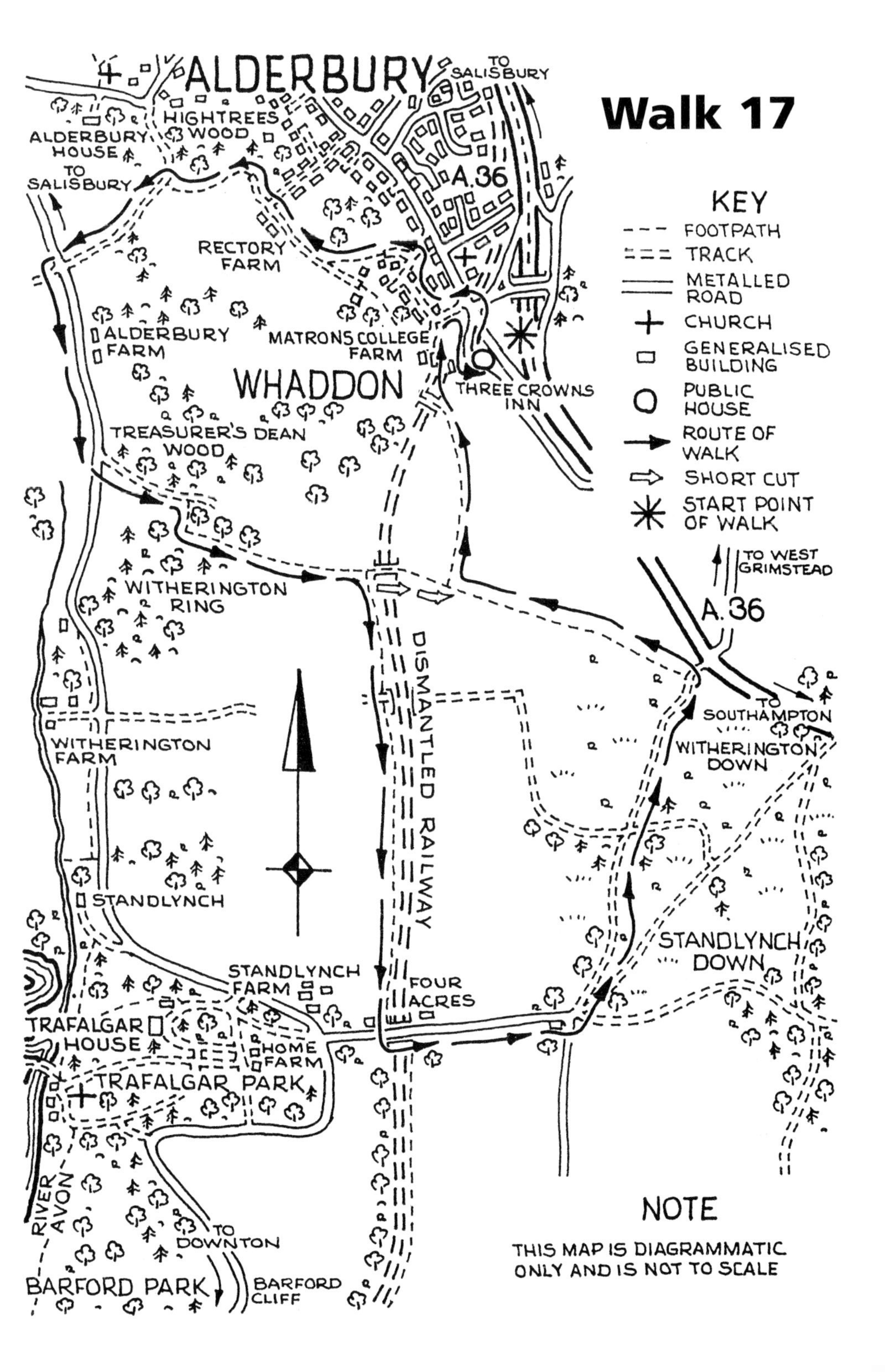
Walk 17
ALDERBURY
TO SALISBURY
HIGHTREES WOOD
ALDERBURY HOUSE
TO SALISBURY
A.36
RECTORY FARM
ALDERBURY FARM
MATRONS COLLEGE FARM
WHADDON
THREE CROWNS INN
TREASURER'S DEAN WOOD
WITHERINGTON RING
DISMANTLED RAILWAY
TO WEST GRIMSTEAD
A.36
TO SOUTHAMPTON
WITHERINGTON DOWN
WITHERINGTON FARM
STANDLYNCH
STANDLYNCH DOWN
STANDLYNCH FARM
FOUR ACRES
TRAFALGAR HOUSE
HOME FARM
TRAFALGAR PARK
RIVER AVON
TO DOWNTON
BARFORD PARK
BARFORD CLIFF
KEY
FOOTPATH
TRACK
METALLED ROAD
CHURCH
GENERALISED BUILDING
PUBLIC HOUSE
ROUTE OF WALK
SHORT CUT
START POINT OF WALK
NOTE
THIS MAP IS DIAGRAMMATIC ONLY AND IS NOT TO SCALE

bends right and three unmetalled tracks diverge left. Take the middle one of these latter, and where this soon forks at the foot of Standlynch Down turn left to follow a hard-surfaced track with trees on either side. Beyond a dip where water collects in wet weather — it can be bypassed — you reach a track-crossing and emerge from wayside woodland into the open.

Trees frame a typical hillscape on the walk from Whaddon

A fenced chalk track leads on ahead, climbing Witherington Down towards the A36 and its traffic. Within yards of this road turn left where a gate and a gap in the fence on that side give access to a bridleway which follows the north margin of arable downland, with a low hedge and fence to your right. Here are the finest views on this walk, extending from Pepperbox Hill behind you across the undulating chalk downland and intervening Avon Valley to Clearbury Ring and its neighbouring high ground away to the west, now ahead of you.

Carry on west along the field-edge to a gate through the hedge at its far corner. Pass through this to follow the left-hand edge of farmland for a short distance before turning right to follow the unfenced grass track previously mentioned as the way back to Whaddon for those on the shorter route. After crossing a hump of arable downland this track descends and angles left, with a fence on your right.

The ivy-mantled brick parapet of a one-time railway arch precedes a gate where a waymarking arrow points out the direction now to be followed, along a right-curving track over pastureland to the left of farm buildings. This brings you to a gate where there are two signs, one of which says 'public bridleway' and the other 'permissive path'. These surely contradict each other. Anyway, carry on through the gate to follow the right-hand edge of the next pasture to the next gate, through which you pass to join a farm road.

Follow this left-handed to turn right at a T-junction with the road along which you first set out, by the sign pointing out the Pack Path — presumably one of those routes once used by packmen hawking their wares in remote country districts in the days when wheeled transport except on roads between the larger towns was a rarity. When you reach the next road opposite the newsagent's shop, turn right, then after a few yards fork right to follow the metalled path leading directly back to The Three Crowns and your car.

Chalkland Heights near Redlynch

WALK 18
Up to 4 hours
5 1/2 miles
Walk begins page 111

Background to the Walk

Redlynch is the centrepiece of a complex of small villages east of the Avon, between Wiltshire's Downton and the Wiltshire-Hampshire border, which also marks the New Forest's northern boundary at this point. With names such as Morgan's Vale, North Charford, Hatchet Green, Hale, Bohemia and the ever intriguing Lover, these villages — some are mere hamlets — virtually adjoin each other while also contributing to the scattered nature of local development as a whole. Newhouse at Redlynch is a Jacobean house periodically opened to the public but there is not much else of historical note in the immediate vicinity. The parish Church of St Birinus, at Morgan's Vale, was built in 1894 at a time when local population was expanding fairly significantly and domestic building likewise.

While also partaking in many respects of the character of a typical Forest-edge village, Redlynch is almost as much a place of the Wiltshire chalk on whose edge it lies. This walk is essentially a chalk walk, with all this promises in terms of well-rounded hillscapes, valley views, hazy skylines and gentle agricultural countryside interspersed with burgeoning woodland abundantly populated with pheasants. Only one footpath stile is encountered, the route being largely one of those that make use of unmetalled lanes and bridleways in an area where human habitations are thin on the ground. Pleasant scenery and rural tranquillity can be looked forward to almost throughout, though peace is briefly interrupted when you cross and recross A36 near the crown of Pepperbox Hill.

You do so on your way to and from The Pepperbox

Maps
Landranger 1:50,000
Sheet 184
Pathfinder 1:25,000
Sheets SU 02/12 and SU22/32
Map Reference of Start/Finish
SU203213

How to get there
Redlynch lies on and adjacent to B3080 just over 1 mile east of Downton and nearly 2 miles from B3080's junction with A338, the Bournemouth-Ringwood-Salisbury road. From Southampton head west along A3024, M271 and M27 to Cadnam, from which follow B3079 to Brook, B3078 across the north of the New Forest to Bramshaw Telegraph and there fork right to follow B3080. Entering Wiltshire, this passes through Woodfalls to reach Redlynch, where you turn right to follow Grove Lane, a few hundred yards along which The King's Head lies on your left. From Bournemouth follow Wessex Way and A338 to Ringwood, where you briefly join eastbound A31 before resuming A338, bypassing Fordingbridge en route to Downton, where you turn right to follow B3080. Within 2 miles turn left at Redlynch to follow Grove Lane for a few hundred yards to The King's Head, on your left. Wilts &

Dorset buses on service X7 from Southampton and service X3 from Poole and Bournemouth connect at Salisbury and Downton respectively with services 43 and 44 to Woodfalls and service 45 to Woodfalls and Hale. Alight at Morgan's Vale crossroads and turn left to follow Grove Lane downhill to The King's Head, on your left as already indicated.

Pub facilities
King's Head
Run by former model Barbara Watkins, this 400-year-old hostelry has just about everything a country pub connoisseur could possibly wish for: suitable setting, unspoilt appearance, lengthy history as a pub and the welcoming atmosphere of a place where one can eat and drink enjoyably — but take care not to bang your head on those low beams! Weekday opening hours are 1200-1430 (until 1500 on Saturdays) and 1800-2300. Sunday hours are as usual. Food may be ordered on weekdays and Sundays from 1200-1400 and on weekdays from 1900-2100, but not on Sunday evenings. Sunday lunchtime roasts are a great favourite as an extra to the regular food menu, which ranges from three different kinds of ploughman's and baked jacket potatoes to soup of the day, cod with chips and garden peas or salad, bacon, steak and chips with baked beans or egg, jumbo sausage with chips, baked beans or egg, and jumbo sausage in a roll. Toasted sandwiches of six different kinds, macaroni cheese, meat or seafood lasagne and seafood pie are also featured, as are prawn

itself. From an altitude of 512 feet above sea level, this hexagonal brick tower, with its pyramidal roof, is a prominent landmark from miles around and a focal point of much curiosity by a ceaseless stream of visitors to the National Trust-owned downland upon the summit of which it looms. It is also known as Eyre's Folly from the probability of its having been erected by Giles Eyre, who died in 1655 and was 'a man much oppressed by public power' — or so says a tablet in his memory in Whiteparish church, two miles to the east.

Built in 1606, The Pepperbox (so-called from its shape) originally had six open arches spaced around its lower storey, with two windows, now blocked in, above each arch. Squire Eyre is supposed to have had it constructed out of envy of the towers of Longford Castle, in the nearby Avon Valley, but not perhaps solely as a 'folly' in the usual sense of a structure purely intended to round off a view and catch the eye. It is thought to have served a practical purpose, perhaps as a sheltered lookout point from which ladies could watch the progress of the hunt when hounds were operating near by. It looks to have been ideal in all respects for such a facility.

Without The Pepperbox as a focus of unending fascination, perhaps the downland round about would not have survived in its present form as a pristine tract of unimproved grassland with associated flora, officially designated now as a Site of Special Scientific Interest (SSSI). The first steps to ensure this were taken in 1934 when a public appeal was launched and land was given by local magnates. In 1949 the 5th Earl Nelson rounded this off with a gift of The Pepperbox itself. Thus it was that Brickworth Down and West Dean Hill became a property of the National Trust and a place where botanists can still hope to find floral treasures like the harebell and the bee orchid as well as typical shrubs of the chalk such as juniper, spindle and wayfaring tree.

For the rest, people come here for the fresh air and the views, which extend to the Isle of Wight in clear weather and encompass much of the New Forest, while in the opposite direction Salisbury nestles in its valley. A view indicator erected by students of Salisbury and South Wilts College of Further Education gives mileages to surrounding places ranging from Andover and Winchester to Southampton, Bournemouth and Shaftesbury, not all of which are visible even on days wholly free of mist.

cocktail, smoked mackerel with salad, Scotch sirloin steak with mushrooms, mixed grill with fried egg, home made steak and kidney pie, half a tender chicken charcoal grilled, and breaded golden scampi. There is also a tempting range of sweets. Ushers' real ales are complemented by three draught lagers, John Smith's Bitter and Scrumpy Jack draught cider. There is a darts room but no jukebox, a pleasant garden for the warmer months and two log fires in winter, a family clientele being catered for. Walkers using the pub may leave their cars in the pub car park — but please ask first.

Walk 18

Distance: ***Allow 4 hours for this five-and-a-half mile walk.***

Leaving The King's Head behind you on your left, head east along the adjoining road for a little way before turning left to follow unmetalled Sandy Lane. Houses flank this as it rises to a stile on your left, which you cross to follow the right-hand edge of a pasture, still heading uphill. A gate brings you out on to a lane which you follow right-handed past Templeman's Old Farmhouse, which lies to your right.

At this point the lane becomes gravelled and hedged with hazels as it heads into typical chalk country. A gently rolling pattern of large arable fields, thick hedgerows and patches of woodland spreads to the east, while to the west, as you gain altitude, the ground dips gently towards the Avon. The whole is suffused with a sense of remoteness. With not a human dwelling in sight once Templeman's Farm is well behind you, nor a single motor car within earshot, this is a countryside where anyone seeking a break from urban bustle can feel wholly at peace with the world.

Nearly a mile beyond the farmhouse you come to a crossing of unmetalled tracks. Here you keep left-ahead to follow a rutted green lane which rises between tall hazel hedgerows. Gaps in the greenery to your left give increasingly scenic westerly views. Beyond the valley of the Avon, Clearbury Ring's topnotch of timber is a dominating landmark which reasserts its prominence every time you look that way.

Reaching a point where woodland flanks the right-hand side of the track, we

paused to demolish picnic sandwiches while enjoying the undulating chalkscape. Pheasants spilled out from wayside hedgerows and a roe deer briefly foraged in the open while we watched. This is a spot where one could enjoyably soak up the scenery for hours.

Follow the green lane north through wood-edge beeches to where a gravel track emerges from the timber to your right. With gravel now underfoot, you keep straight on to a T-junction of gravel roads. Turn left here, then where the gravel road dips left within a few yards bear right to climb past a high ground reservoir. Once woodland passes behind, views open out as you head north along a fenced grass- and chalk-surfaced track. This converges with another track from your left as you approach a gate beyond which your track leads on through trees to reach A36 at the top of Pepperbox Hill.

Cross this wide and very busy road with great care to follow a hollow chalk track directly opposite. This leads to a car park close to The Pepperbox, having inspected which walk on a few yards farther, left-ahead, to where a direction indicator measures the miles to various places. In all but the murkiest of weather you should be able to see as far as Southampton Water in one direction and well beyond Salisbury in the other. To the south a dark smudge of dense timber announces the New Forest's northerly high ground, while another broad mass of woodlands clothes much of the lower land to the north, beyond which the chalk plateau of Salisbury Plain rears on the skyline.

If time and energy permit, take a leisurely stroll over Brickworth Down to seek out some of those floral delights which have helped to give it special status in the sphere of conservation. Then turn about to head back towards Redlynch, recrossing A36 where you did previously and then retracing your steps along the chalk track

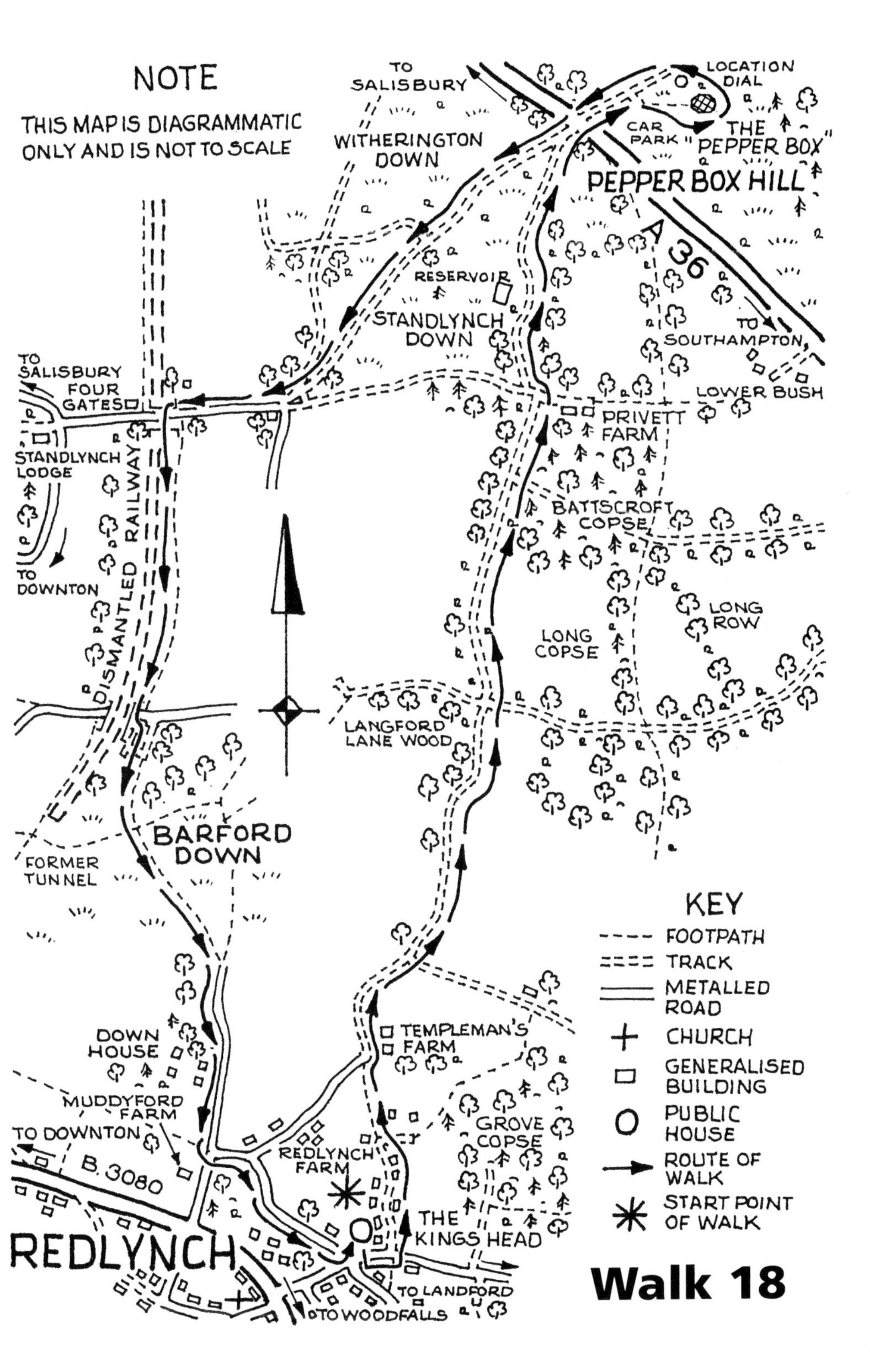
NOTE
THIS MAP IS DIAGRAMMATIC ONLY AND IS NOT TO SCALE
TO SALISBURY
WITHERINGTON DOWN
LOCATION DIAL
CAR PARK
"THE PEPPER BOX"
PEPPER BOX HILL
A 36
TO SOUTHAMPTON
RESERVOIR
STANDLYNCH DOWN
TO SALISBURY
FOUR GATES
STANDLYNCH LODGE
TO DOWNTON
DISMANTLED RAILWAY
LOWER BUSH
PRIVETT FARM
BATTSCROFT COPSE
LONG ROW
LONG COPSE
LANGFORD LANE WOOD
BARFORD DOWN
FORMER TUNNEL
TEMPLEMAN'S FARM
DOWN HOUSE
MUDDYFORD FARM
TO DOWNTON
B. 3080
REDLYNCH FARM
GROVE COPSE
THE KINGS HEAD
REDLYNCH
TO LANDFORD
TO WOODFALLS
KEY
FOOTPATH
TRACK
METALLED ROAD
CHURCH
GENERALISED BUILDING
PUBLIC HOUSE
ROUTE OF WALK
START POINT OF WALK

Walk 18

The way north from Redlynch

opposite. After passing through the gate a few yards along this, fork right from the track you followed on the outward stage of this walk to follow a grassy track which rises briefly before angling downhill and presenting dramatic views across the Avon Valley, to your right.

Towards the foot of a half-mile descent you pass through trees to reach a metalled lane at a point where it bends sharply. Passing an isolated lodge-type cottage on your left, follow the metalled lane right-handed, downhill, to the near side of where it bridges a tree-filled cutting where trains once ran. Here turn left by a bridleway signpost indicating the way to Redlynch to pass through a gate and follow a track along the right-hand edge of farmland. The bushed-in course of the old Salisbury-West Moors railway lies to your right as you head south, traversing three successive field margins before reaching another road with a tree-topped old railway arch to your right.

Angle left to cross the road and follow a grassy, hedged bridleway. Trees overhang this as it veers away from the former railway, diagonally climbing a ridge of chalk downland before following the right-hand edge of a field to converge with a chalk track which becomes a narrow, hedged lane as you follow it to the right. Take the first metalled lane that turns left from this, and where this soon forks bear right to follow a byway called The Row. This reaches Redlynch at a crossroads within yards of The King's Head, which lies directly to your left.

Ancient Forest Ways near Hamptworth

WALK 19
Allow 3 hours
4 1/2, 5 or 6 miles
Walk begins page 117

Background to the Walk

Hamptworth's two syllables seem to duplicate each other's meaning and probably refer to an enclosed settlement once flanked by commonland on at least three sides: Hamptworth Common, Landford Common and North Common respectively. Hamptworth today is a scattered agricultural hamlet amid the heavily wooded countryside that extends several miles into south-east Wiltshire from the New Forest, with which it shares a number of features, including typical forest wildlife. Deer, for example, are no respecters of either forest or county boundaries and may be found in all these woods. We saw the fresh hoofmarks of fallow deer on farmland less than a quarter-of-a-mile from The Cuckoo Inn.

Landford dates back to Domesday, 20 years after the Norman Conquest, when it was recorded as 'Langeford'. By AD1242 it had dropped a 'g' to become 'Laneford', which seems to describe it to a nicety as signifying 'a ford crossed by a lane'. At that time Landford was within the Forest of Melchet which, with adjoining Clarendon Forest, formed a continuous royal hunting preserve linking up with the New Forest and extending almost to Salisbury.

The Landford of today consists in the main of modern dwellings in the midst of former commonland reclaimed for agriculture. This erstwhile open grazing ground is overlooked from a hilltop just beyond A36 by the parish Church of St Andrew, a bell-towered, stone-and-brick edifice in the Early English style which was rebuilt in 1858 on the site of a very much older church. Indeed, there has probably been a church at

Maps
Landranger 1:50,000
Sheet 184
Pathfinder 1:25,000
Sheets SU 21/31 & SU 22/32
Map Reference of Start/Finish
SU242198

How to get there
The Cuckoo Inn *at Hamptworth lies on the Landford-Redlynch road, 1 mile west of Landford which is on B3079, the road that runs west and north from Cadnam by way of Brook to join A36 a mile west of Plaitford. To reach Hamptworth From Southampton follow A3024, M271, westbound M27, ands then A36, from which you turn left for Landford about 1 mile after passing tThe Shoe Inn at Plaitford and entering Wiltshire. At the next T-junction turn left, then take first right for Hamptworth. From Bournemouth follow Wessex Waay and A338 to Ringwoiod, there briefly joining eastbound A31 before resuming A338, from which you turn right at Downton to follow B3080 east for 2 miles before turning left at Redlynch, beyond which you disregard a subsequent left turn for Whiteparish to reach The Cuckoo Inn almost 3 miles farther on. Landford, an alternative starting point, is*

served by Wilts & Dorset limited stop buses on service X7 between Southampton, Totton, Plaitford and Salisbury and by Wilts & Dorset buses on service 39 between Romsey, Bramshaw and Fritham, which extends to Hamptworth on certain days.

Pub facilities
The Cuckoo Inn
This is an old style country pub 'in the middle of nowhere', and looks the part with its come-hither combination of thatch and brick and its two bars totally uncluttered by townee trappings of any sort. This free house opens between 1130-1430 and 1800-2300 from Mondays to Fridays, all day Saturdays and at the usual times on Sundays and offers a choice of 10 real ales including Merrie Monk Mild, Tanglefoot, Farmer's Glory, Bass, Wadworth 6X, Badger Best, Mitchell's, Henry Wadworth IPA and King Alfred as well as a guest beer of the month. Taunton Traditional Dry Cider is also on tap. Bar snacks are always available and include rolls, ploughman's and pasties. Barbecues are a summer attraction. There is a garden and a play area for children. Dogs on leads are admitted and walkers using the pub may use the pub car park. The pub fields a cricket team and petanque is played here. Darts, dominoes and quiz nights all contribute to a lively social atmosphere enjoyed by both regulars and visitors. The building dates from the turn of the century and at one time included a shop.

this spot since before the Norman Conquest. Embodied in the fabric of the present church is a stone reputedly of Saxon origin bearing the figures of two priests. This was found in the foundations of the chancel of the previous church and is in the west wall of the present one, by the entrance.

Apart from what used to be Landford Common, the southerly view from Landford churchyard extends to Bramshaw Wood, in the Forest, on the skyline and is one of the finest in the area. Tall-chimneyed Landford Manor House, next door, is a notable landmark. Built about 1600, it was originally gabled but was extensively altered during the reign of Queen Anne. On the wall of an upstair room is a representation in oak of a naked lady with two knights which was transferred there from the previous Landford church when this was demolished in 1856. No doubt Victorian church builders were only too glad to disembarrass themselves of such an unseemly ornament. The manor house remained a private residence until the 1930s and is nowadays the headquarters of a cartographical enterprise.

Landfordwood, to the north, is a scattered residential area two miles from the centre of Landford proper. It occupies part of the old Melchet Court estate, which was broken up in 1936. Melchet Court itself is now a special school. Melchet Park, in which it lies, is of very ancient origin. Once surrounded by the Royal Forest of Melchet, it was a mediaeval deer park in its own right. During the reign of Henry II his Chief Justice of the Forest, Alan de Neville, is recorded as having 'broken the park of Melchet', which 'caused the deer to go out', no doubt to the great annoyance of the local farming community whose crops the escapees would make free with.

On the opposite side of the A36 from Landfordwood is Earldoms, a wooded area which in 1552 was granted to the then Earl of Pembroke. You will pass through this if you follow the six-mile version of this walk, or skirt just south of it at Northlands if the five-mile route is your choice.

At the time when we did this walk the River Blackwater, a Test tributary which flows from west to east through the parish of Landford, seemed likely to be accepted as a natural northern boundary of the New Forest Heritage Area, planned to embrace some borderland areas as well as the Forest proper. Local opinion, however, strongly favoured a more northerly limit still, to include the whole of Landford parish and, hence, the church and its scenic surroundings.

Cuckoo Inn, Hamptworth

Walk 19

Distance: ***Allow up to 3 hours for the four-and-a-half, five or six mile walks.***

There are two alternative starts to this walk, with little to choose between them in terms of distance. The very slightly longer one is to head west along the road from The Cuckoo Inn for a few yards to where a footpath sign points through a gap in the hedge by a broken gate to your left. From here, heading more or less at right-angles from the road, you cross an arable field to pass through another hedge gap and enter a second field, the left-hand edge of which you follow. Where this soon bends right, stay with it, with a wood on your left-hand side. It was here that we saw fallow deer hoofmarks: a salutary reminder that the New Forest and its fauna are only a couple of miles distant from this south-east Wiltshire farmland.

Halfway along the length of the wood another path crosses your own, Follow the new path left-handed into the wood, just inside which we had to circumvent obstruction from a windblown tree before proceeding along what turned out to be a well-defined and otherwise clear path through the encompassing timber. Emerging from the wood, you join and follow left-handed a lane which is joined from the right within yards by another lane. A hundred yards or so farther on turn right to follow a gravel lane — which can also be reached by turning left as you leave The Cuckoo Inn and then immediately turning right to follow the cottage-bordered Nomansland road. From this you turn left within 200 yards to follow the gravel lane just mentioned, which is a public bridleway.

This unmetalled lane fords a stream at a watersplash which is bypassed on the left by a wooden footbridge, having crossed which you resume what is now a tree-shaded track of earth and gravel. Heading east, within a mile you emerge on to B3079 at Landford, an alternative place to start the walk for those who are using public transport. Here two more alternatives present themselves to walkers. The first is to follow the village road right-handed for about 200 yards to the end of a wood on your left, and there turn left to follow a gravel road signposted to Landford Fruit Farm.

Where the gravelled way soon bends right, keep straight on along the left-hand edge of cultivated ground with a hedge to your left. This leads to a stile which you cross to follow the left-hand edge of a pasture to where the field-edge angles half-right. Here you cross on your left a stile with a rickety step and then a plank bridge, immediately beyond which you bear left where a weatherworn sign points out the footpath. If you miss this and continue ahead you may soon meet folk who will not be happy about your being on private property, although the A36 is reachable this way. The footpath proper leads to another stile beyond which it skirts to the right of a garden centre. You next pass round a metal gate to follow the right-hand edge of a paddock to a footbridge over a ditch followed by a stile leading out on to A36, the busy Southampton-Salisbury main road.

Turn right and then left to cross the main road and follow a farm drive as far as a house on your right, about 100 yards along. The official footpath continues ahead past outbuildings to follow a partially obstructed course to a semi-derelict footbridge over the River Blackwater. This is just about crossable by an athlete who might be prepared to risk a ducking. A better bet, however, unless the footbridge has been repaired or renewed and the footpath obstructions cleared by the time you tackle this walk, is to cross iron railings on your left directly opposite the house and then follow the right-hand edge of an arable field to a much more robust farm bridge a few yards left of the bridge last mentioned. This is acceptable, we were told, in view of the river crossing problem presented by the official footpath.

Carry on ahead to follow the left-hand edge of a pasture uphill to a gate and stile followed by a rising track towards Landford Manor Farm buildings, with Landford Manor House on your left. Here you emerge on to a lane which you follow left-handed for a few yards to St Andrew's Church and the view it commands across surrounding countryside. We sat on a churchyard seat in the sunshine to enjoy our picnic lunch before backtracking to Landford village to check out an alternative route which avoids diverging from the official right of way at any point.

Combined with the road instead of the footpath approach from The Cuckoo Inn to the Hamptworth-Landford bridleway already described, this shortens the five-mile route overall by half-a-mile. When you reach Lyndhurst Road (B3079) at Landford, cross it to follow a left-turning metalled footpath behind the houses there, with fields on your right-hand side. This path re-emerges alongside the road, which you follow ahead for a short distance to a crescent of houses called Brookside. Leaving the road at this point, cross the green in front of the houses to pass a footpath sign on your left before joining a fenced path between a pasture on your right and a wooded gully in which flows the River Blackwater on your left.

We found this path profusely grown with summer herbage which we had to beat aside with sticks at certain points to clear a way through. It leads to a stile where an arrowed waymark keeps you on course as you follow the left edge of the next pasture to a farmyard. Here you follow some bordering railings to your right for a few yards to cross a metal-barred, wooden-stepped stile. A gravel track now leads you between the farmhouse and the outbuildings of Bridge Farm to another stile, beyond which you emerge on to A36. Follow the main road left-handed to cross the River Blackwater and then immediately turn right to follow a hollow lane uphill to Landford church and Landford Manor.

Here the alternative routes reunite as you carry on past the church and the manor house to a stile on the right-hand side of the lane, which here bends left. Cross the stile and head where the footpath sign here directs, across a pasture to a second stile, after crossing which you turn right, with a bushed-in track to your left and a fence to your right. Your path emerges by way of a track alongside a house to join a rough-surfaced road which you follow left-handed through a gate, past scattered dwellings and through fields to a T-junction of lanes in Landfordwood. Houses flank the lane you now follow left, soon passing between stone pillars where once was a gated entrance to the grounds of Melchet Court. There was a corresponding entrance from Sherfield English, just inside Hampshire, the one you see here being in Wiltshire.

The lane you now follow skirts a small wood into which a signposted footpath turns right, offering an alternative middle section of the walk which will make the whole route a six-miler. For the slightly shorter version, after leaving Landfordwood carry on along Stock Lane, as the byway serving this outlying part of Landford proper is called. On being joined from the right by a metalled driveway after skirting the wood last mentioned, the lane bends left to reach A36. Cross this busy road with great care and climb a diagonal metalled path to reach a section of the old main road which was bypassed when A36 was widened and straightened here. Cross the old road and head right-handed to join and follow gravelled North Common Lane past the scattered dwellings of Northlands. Fields stretch to not-far-distant woods beside this lane as you follow it west. After crossing a tree-bordered headstream of the River Blackwater you carry on by North Common Farm, where barking dogs may salute your passing. Go through a metal gate and follow a woodland track ahead to a crossing of tracks in a valley, where the longer middle section and the shorter walk reunite. Those who are following the short route should turn hard left here.

If you opt for the longer walk, follow the signposted woodland path which turns right-handed from the lane just after leaving Landfordwood. A few yards along it the well-defined path divides and here you fork left. Soon you emerge from the trees on to a metalled lane opposite a plant depot. Follow the lane right-handed for a few yards, then turn left to follow a grass-centred track with the plant depot now on your left and a garden on your right. This brings you to a gate alongside a stile with a waymarking arrow. Cross the stile and follow the arrow to head diagonally right across a meadow. Go through or over a metal gate halfway along the length of the field fence now ahead of you, then continue across

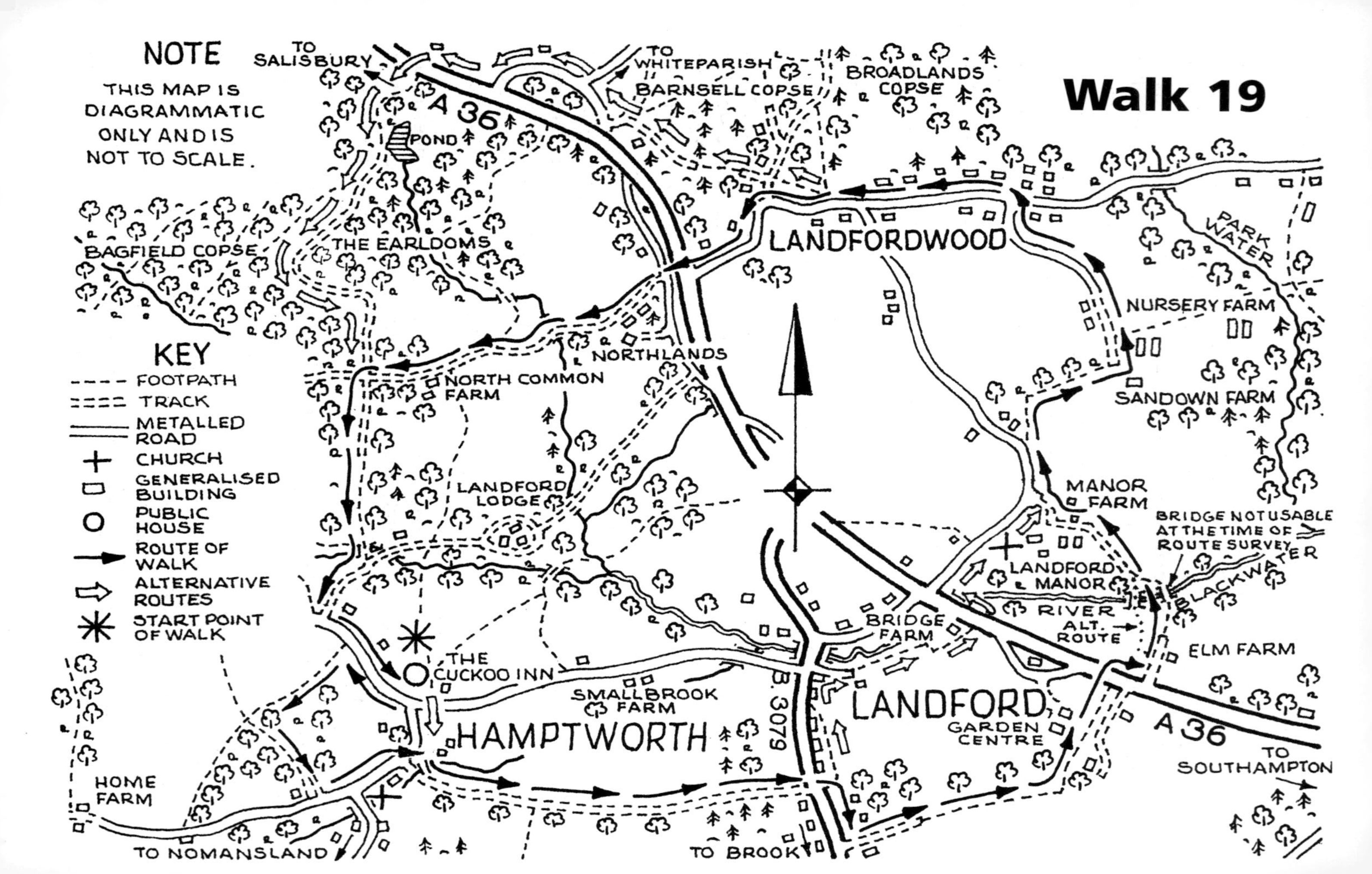
Walk 19
NOTE
THIS MAP IS DIAGRAMMATIC ONLY AND IS NOT TO SCALE.
KEY
FOOTPATH
TRACK
METALLED ROAD
CHURCH
GENERALISED BUILDING
PUBLIC HOUSE
ROUTE OF WALK
ALTERNATIVE ROUTES
START POINT OF WALK
TO SALISBURY
A 36
POND
TO WHITEPARISH
BARNSELL COPSE
BROADLANDS COPSE
BAGFIELD COPSE
THE EARLDOMS
LANDFORDWOOD
PARK WATER
NURSERY FARM
SANDOWN FARM
NORTHLANDS
NORTH COMMON FARM
LANDFORD LODGE
MANOR FARM
BRIDGE NOT USABLE AT THE TIME OF ROUTE SURVEY
BLACKWATER
LANDFORD MANOR
RIVER
ALT. ROUTE
BRIDGE FARM
ELM FARM
THE CUCKOO INN
SMALLBROOK FARM
B.3079
LANDFORD
GARDEN CENTRE
A 36
TO SOUTHAMPTON
HAMPTWORTH
HOME FARM
TO NOMANSLAND
TO BROOK

the next meadow to a broken stile with another waymarking arrow.

This precedes a path fenced on the right and with scrub woodland and rhododendrons on the left of it. If you have to lift the broken stile aside to follow this path, remember to replace it afterwards to prevent farm stock from straying. Your path soon joins a grass-centred track emerging from the left, and along this you continue ahead to where it becomes a gravel driveway serving various dwellings. Carry on along this to join and follow ahead a metalled remnant of the old A36 before its once twisty course hereabouts was straightened. This joins the Earldoms-Whiteparish road, which you follow left-handed. A few yards short of where this joins A36 you follow a scrub-bordered right-hand track — another fragment of the old main road — to reach and cross the busy highway a little way farther west.

Follow the grass verge of A36 west for a few yards to a point directly opposite Glendale Farm, which lies to your right. Turn left here to follow an unsignposted track into dense woodland which the map reveals as extending for some three miles without a break: a sizeable chunk of the forest which once clothed much of south-east Wiltshire. Where the track soon forks, keep right. The track you now follow curves left to skirt right-handed of the grounds of Earldoms Lodge and of a half-hidden wood-edge pond. Just ahead now you ford a winding woodland brook — no problem in dry summer weather for those wearing shoes instead of boots — to carry on along a grass ride with well-grown timber trees to your left and the old hazel coppice of an area called Glazier's Copse to your right. The woodland to your left is called The Earldoms, recalling a time when an Earl of Pembroke had an interest in this neighbourhood.

Although no longer blessed with the title 'forest', this complex of coppices and plantations between the A36 and Redlynch remains a haunt of much forest wildlife. There have probably always been deer in these deep woods, and you will see signs of them in the form of well-worn ruts marking their crossing-points of ancient coppice banks, though perhaps not the elusive beasts themselves, at many points along this secluded section of the walk.

Where the ride forks keep straight on along a grass ride which continues ahead for half-a-mile or so and then circles left around a dark conifer grove to a junction of tracks on the woodland's edge. Turn right here to follow a track with meadowland on your left and woodland, at first, on your right, followed by pasture.

The oak-and-hazel-hedged track leads you ahead to a valley track-crossing at the end of the right-hand pasture, not many yards west of North Common Farm, where you rejoin the shorter route and keep straight on.

You soon reach a stile beyond which you follow the right-hand edge of a pasture and an area of replanted trees to another stile followed by a bridge over one of the River Blackwater's headstreams. Here you join and follow right-handed a grass-centred lane which climbs between hedges to join the Redlynch-Landford road. Follow this left-handed past Hamptworth's Old Post Office Cottages, with their thatch and herringbone brickwork, to arrive back at The Cuckoo Inn, where you started.

Wooded Ways around Minstead

WALK 20
Allow 3 hours
5 miles
Walk begins page 124

Background to the Walk

Minstead is one of those communities which seem emphatically set apart from the outside world. Except for a tenuous link with Lyndhurst's surrounding fields and other enclosed land, it is completely encircled by forest and it is this, above all else, that makes it a little world apart, insulated from inappropriate, alien influences.

The *Victoria County History*, that unique window on Hampshire life as lived in the early years of the 20th century, refers to Minstead as a village of 'scattered deep roofed thatched cottages', and it is still such a place today. Modern building has intruded little. Picturesque ancient dwellings pop up around almost every corner: the enduring embodiment of an age-old way of life linked with the fields around and with the all-embracing Forest.

Yet all is not as it may seem. Pausing by one picture-postcard cottage to write up some notes on the walk, my companion and I attracted suspicion. The owner's enquiry whether we needed help had more to do with satisfying himself that we had no ulterior motives than with offering assistance. There had been, he said, a number of recent burglaries, with cottages like his own, no longer the homes of humble peasants but of people with possessions, being singled out for special attention.

Minstead, in the main, has had a long, untroubled history since that one event which sealed it in public memory — the death by an arrow loosed accidentally or on purpose, supposedly at nearby Canterton Glen, of William Rufus while hunting one August day in

Maps
Landranger 1:50,000
Sheet 195
Pathfinder 1:25,000
or Outdoor Leisure Map
Map Reference of Start/
Finish: SU282110

How to get there
From Southampton follow A3024, A35, Totton's southern and western bypasses and A336 via Netley Marsh before forking left for Bartley. At Bartley crossroads continue ahead into the New Forest, crossing A337 and then almost immediately forking left. At the next crossroads join a road which bends right as you follow it right-handed. The Trusty Servant Inn is on your left by the next turning. If you turn left here you may find alternative parking space outside Minstead church, at the top of the hill. From Bournemouth follow Wessex Way east, A338 and then A31 to the beginning of M27 at Cadnam, where you turn off and take the third exit from the slip road. At the next roundabout take the third exit to follow A337 towards Lyndhurst, at the first crossroads along which you turn right. Directions thenceforward are as from Southampton after crossing

AD1100. Whether this was the actual scene of the slaying is still disputed and will probably never be settled, although the iron plaque on Rufus's Stone hints at no doubts upon the matter.

Recorded in Domesday as 'Mintestede', meaning 'a place where mint is grown', there was probably a church here as well as a village in Saxon times. The present Church of All Saints, on its little, secluded hill not very far south of the village pub, owes something to various periods dating back at least to the 13th century and was originally thatched. It has several highly distinctive characteristics, not least its triangular arrangement of nave, chancel and a side chapel or secondary nave which almost exceeds the nave proper in dimensions. Georgian family pews for the local gentry, galleries once used by church musicians and to seat the parish poor including children from a local charity school, a 17th century three-decker pulpit, a font with a pre-Norman basin, a Norman chancel arch and a rare pre-Reformation church bell are other features, all adding up to a singularly delightful if decidedly unusual Hampshire village church interior.

The double lych-gate is modern, but the churchyard yew has been shown by a ring count to be around 400 years old. The ring count was made possible by some necessary surgery, the evidence of which is sadly all too plain to see.

Gravestones in the churchyard include at least one of a Purkess. It was a charcoal-burner named Purkess who is supposed to have carted the body of William Rufus to Winchester for burial, and the surname has remained common in the New Forest to this day. Also buried in the churchyard are various Comptons, a family whose heads were lords of Minstead manor for several centuries and who lived, as one would expect, in the Manor House. Another Minstead mansion, Castle Malwood, was built in 1892, taking its name from an ancient earthwork in the northern part of the area, the name Malwood being associated with that of Godric de Malf, who apparently held land here during the reign of Edward the Confessor. Castle Malwood is now the headquarters of Southern Electric.

Perhaps the best known Minstead resident of recent

A337. Solent Blue Line/Wilts & Dorset bus services 31 and 31A from Southampton pass through Minstead en route to Lyndhurst. From Bournemouth take Wilts & Dorset service X2 to Cadnam and change there to Solent Blue Line/Wilts & Dorset service 31 or 31A.

Pub facilities
Trusty Servant Inn
This well-known hostelry, with its sign depicting a hog-headed retainer with explanatory verse, serves breakfast from 0900-1100 and afternoon tea including cream teas from 1430-1800. Weekday pub hours are 1100-1430 and 1800-2300. Lunchtime bar snacks may be ordered between 1100-1400. Evening restaurant service is from 1800-2130 with a restaurant area seating over 50 people. There is a barn for special functions including barn dances. Overnight accommodation includes 4 double and 2 single rooms. Wadworth 6X and Flower's Original real ales are served. Also on draught are Guinness and Murphy's Irish stout and Stella Artois and Heineken lagers as well as dry and medium white wines and red wine. Regular menu items range from soup of the day with hot crusty bread and butter, smoked trout fillets and horseradish, 6 potato skins filled with bacon and cheese and with blue cheese dip, prawn open sandwiches, deep fried brie and hot toast, crispy whitebait with brown bread and butter, and mussels in garlic wine and cheese sauce to firecracker prawns with hot chilli dip, 3 types of ploughman's with bread,

pickles and salad, ham, egg and chips, Cumberland sausages with chips, deep fried haddock with chips and salad, breaded scampi with chips and salad, and savoury pancake with crispy vegetables, salad and chips. There is also a generous range of daily specials, while the Continental Cafe menu lists full English, Continental or light breakfast as well as a good choice of afternoon and high tea dishes. Children are admitted and a children's menu is available. Pub-using walkers may use the pub car park and there is additional parking space on the other side of the adjacent village green, on which summer fairs and morris dancing periodically take place.

times was the man who created Sherlock Holmes, Sir Arthur Conan Doyle, whose home was at Bignell Wood, on the south side of the road between Brook and Cadnam. Sir Arthur died in 1930 at Windlesham in Surrey but was later reburied at Minstead along with his wife, who died ten years later. Their grave is under an oak tree at the far end of the churchyard.

The building in Minstead which perhaps excites more interest than most others is the pub, The Trusty Servant, with its sign depicting a bipedal pig-headed menial with ass's ears and the hoofs of a stag, attired in the Windsor livery of the time of George III. This is a copy of a portrait which hangs at the kitchen entrance in Winchester College, though it seems there is no special connection between the college and the pub except perhaps a shared sense of humour by individuals linked with each. The swine-snouted character with his padlocked jaw, his wig, his sword and shield and his implements of work as a household servant is supposed to embody all the desirable qualities of a well-schooled retainer as envisaged by an artist of times long past who was also a wit as the appended verse shows.

A Trusty Servant's portrait would you see,
This Emblematic Figure we'll survey.
The Porker's Snout not nice in diet shows,
The Padlock shut no secret he'll disclose.
Patient the Ass his master's wrath will bear,
Swiftness in errand the Stagg's feet declare;
Loaded his left hand apt to labour saith
The Vest his neatness, Open hand his faith.
Girt with his Sword his Shield upon his arm,
Himself and master he'll protect from harm.

The painting from which this was copied dates from 1809 when it replaced a previous painting at least 200 years older. This in turn is thought to have been inspired by a French original, 'Le Chateau de Labour' by Pierre Gringore, first published in 1499. If it was meant mainly as a joke it has certainly stood the test of time.

Walk 20

Distance: ***Allow 3 hours for this five mile walk.***

From The Trusty Servant Inn follow the adjacent side lane uphill towards the church, passing the village green with its war memorial and well on your left. On your right are Crofton Cottages, built in 1897 as a technical school on a site given by the lord of the manor to mark Queen Victoria's Diamond Jubilee.

Spare time to visit the church with its cosy interior, to inspect the churchyard yew and to look for the gravestone of Conan Doyle and other more local

The Trusty Servant pub at Minstead and (right) the pub sign

notabilities before continuing through the kissing-gate to the right of the churchyard entrance. A fenced and hedged footpath leads you south-westward between pastures and through a brief section of Manor Wood, passing through three further kissing-gates before emerging on to a road in an area called Newtown.

After crossing a footbridge to the left of a watersplash ford as you head left-handed along this road, bear left of the road itself to follow a parallel path which soon peters out as a visible footway. You now follow the line of least resistance through old oaks and hollies between a woodland fence on your left and the rear of a dwelling facing the lane to your right. Somewhat squelchy after rain, this brings you out on to a lane which bends right as you follow it left-handed to pass a house called Muffins and a picturesque thatched dwelling, Woodside Cottage, which looks like something straight out of a fairytale. Yew Tree Cottage, not far beyond, is hardly less visually appealing, providing a blind eye is turned to the tiled extension at its rear.

Minstead's Manor Wood lies to your left as you carry on to where your own lane soon joins another. Here bear right and head uphill to a crossing of lanes where you turn left. Now heading downhill, you pass Robins Bush Farm on your right before crossing a footbridge alongside a concreted watersplash ford. Your lane now rises past Acres Down Farm (bed and breakfast, cream teas!). Immediately beyond this, where a gravel track turns left and another continues ahead into the Forest, follow a metalled road right-handed to a fork a few yards ahead, and there turn left to follow a gravel road through hollies, tall oaks and beeches.

This gravelled way veers right-handed to a gate where you enter Highland Water Inclosure, a wood as attractive as its name, thanks to the undulating variety of deciduous trees and conifers, ancient timber and young plantations, fresh and pleasing permutations of which confront you at every turn. Tall, dark pines, rugged Douglas firs and smooth-stemmed beeches, among others, alternate

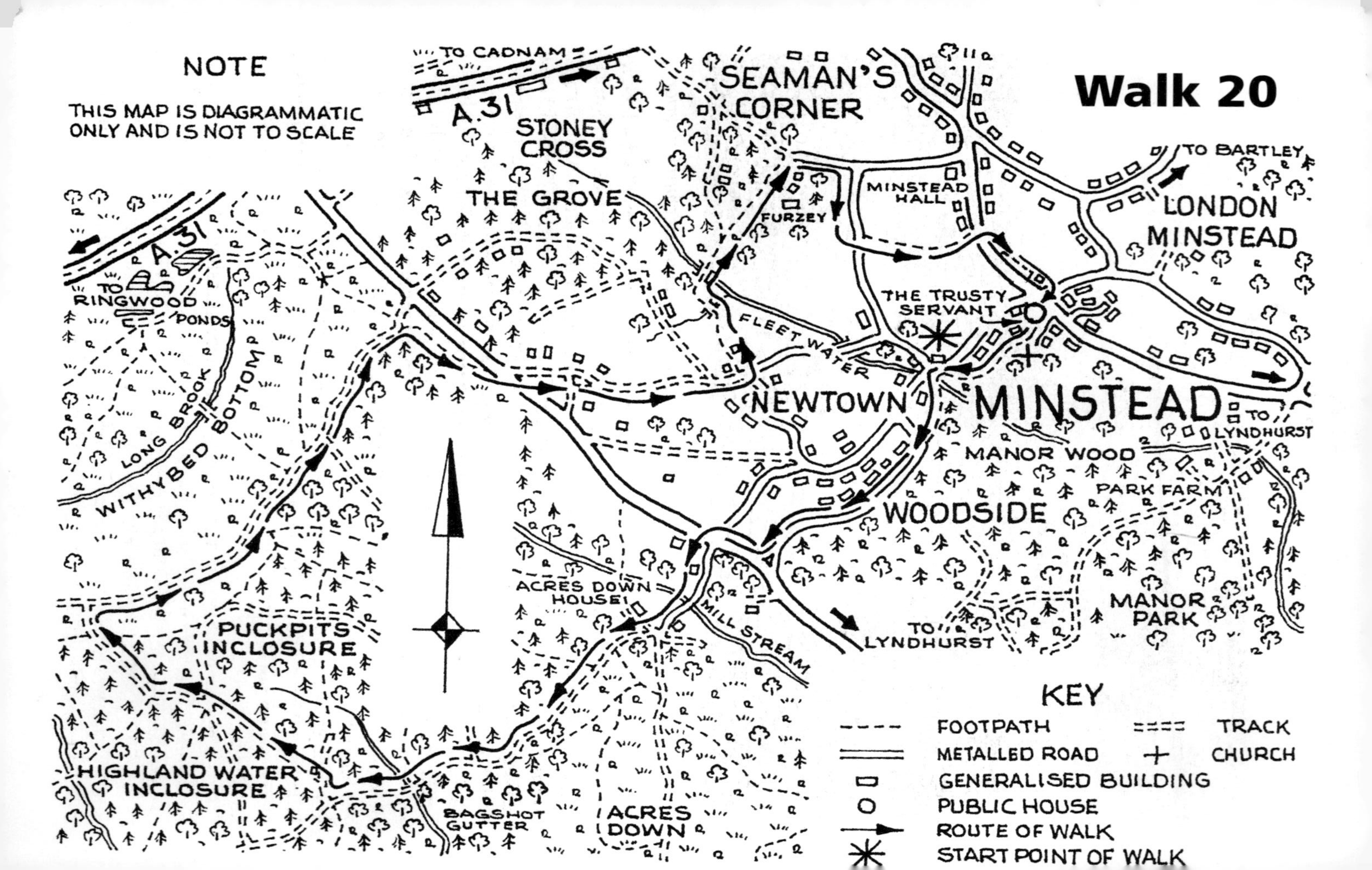

Walk 20
NOTE
THIS MAP IS DIAGRAMMATIC ONLY AND IS NOT TO SCALE
TO CADNAM
A.31
STONEY CROSS
SEAMAN'S CORNER
THE GROVE
FURZEY
MINSTEAD HALL
TO BARTLEY
LONDON MINSTEAD
THE TRUSTY SERVANT
FLEET WATER
NEWTOWN
MINSTEAD
TO LYNDHURST
MANOR WOOD
PARK FARM
WOODSIDE
MANOR PARK
TO LYNDHURST
A.31
TO RINGWOOD
PONDS
LONG BROOK
BOTTOM
WITHYBED
ACRES DOWN HOUSE
MILL STREAM
PUCKPITS INCLOSURE
HIGHLAND WATER INCLOSURE
BAGSHOT GUTTER
ACRES DOWN
KEY
FOOTPATH
TRACK
METALLED ROAD
CHURCH
GENERALISED BUILDING
PUBLIC HOUSE
ROUTE OF WALK
START POINT OF WALK

Church of All Saints, Minstead — a singularly delightful if unusual church interior

alongside the track you follow left to cross Bagshot Bottom, through which flows Bagshot Gutter, a feeder stream of Highland Water. This latter brook turns out to be a youthful Lymington River, a name, however, that it disdains until enlarged by other tributaries, such as Black Water and Ober Water, north of Brockenhurst.

Keeping to the gravel road via which you entered this woodland, carry on past a clear-felled area to where another gravel road turns right, with a woodman's hut to its left just past where an unmetalled ride turns left from it. Follow this latter, heading north-west in a straight line between lofty pines, climbing steadily at first, and then descending to join a gravel road at a point where it is joined in turn by another gravel road, directly opposite the ride from which you now emerge.

Follow the gravel road ahead, with tall pines to the right of it as well as to the left, where the ground slopes down into the valley through which flows the Highland Water, adding up to a scenically sylvan stretch. The gravel road ends at a turn-round point from which you carry on ahead to a gate where you leave the inclosure.

The scene now changes dramatically, with tree-splashed Withybed Bottom forming the base of a heathland amphitheatre which cradles the Highland Water away to your left as you now turn right to follow a well-defined rising track, with the inclosure fence to your right. The far rim of the amphitheatre carries the A31 dual carriageway with its ceaselessly throbbing traffic, as marked a contrast as could be possible with the tranquillity closer to hand.

The grave of Sir Arthur Conan Doyle and his wife Jean

Old oaks and beeches intermittently flank your heathland track as you follow it up and over. Keep to the main track and avoid all minor ones until a house roof backed by a pinewood appears ahead as you emerge from some pine trees. Follow a gravelly path that turns right here through an open forest area of gorse and scrub, converging on a road from your left, which you join and follow ahead to the end of a fenced wood on your left. Here you fork left to follow a signposted gravel bridleway with fenced private property to your left.

By the entrance to a house called King's Garn on your left your track briefly ceases to be gravelled and winds through hollies before emerging and resuming a better surface. Bordering paddocks precede a road, joining which you turn left to cross a stile on your left and follow a signposted, fenced footpath between houses and their gardens. Fairly soon you cross a stream and a stile to follow the left-hand edge of a paddock to a further stile. After crossing the latter turn right, as a yellow waymarking arrow here indicates, then descend through oaks and hollies to a stile and a handrailed plank bridge over a brook here called Fleet Water. This later natures as the Bartley Water to join the Test between Eling and Totton, where it is spanned by an ancient toll-bridge near Eling tide mill.

Beyond this your path veers right and rises between more oaks and hollies, with a fence on your right-hand side. Soon you turn right to pass through a break in the wooden fence you have been following. Your path now leads through yet more oaks and hollies, crosses a stream by another plank bridge and emerges past a footpath sign on to a track which you follow ahead to join and follow right-handed a lane by Furzey Gardens, a thatched and timber-framed cottage where you can get coffee or afternoon tea.

At a triangular T-junction the lane you now follow joins another holly-bordered byway which you follow in its turn to where a footpath sign on your left flanks a stile. Cross this stile to follow the left-hand hedge and fence of a sizeable pasture. A handrailed plank bridge and a stepless stile precede a paddock, the leftward edge of which you follow to a stile leading into a lane. Follow this lane right-handed, taking advantage of a short parallel left-hand footpath before rejoining the metalled byway, which you follow ahead, descending past thatched cottages to a lane crossing where you turn right for The Trusty Servant Inn and the end of this final walk in and around the delightful New Forest. I hope one and all will have given you pleasure and happy memories of one of England's choicest areas.